Building Brands On Purpose

A strategic marketing framework
to win the hearts and minds of your
team and customers, for life

Chris Hogan

R**e**think

First published in Great Britain in 2021 by Rethink Press
(www.rethinkpress.com)

Contents

Introduction

There was a time when I would have introduced myself as the world's worst marketer. It's a strange way to start a story but this was how I felt during the darkest moment of my life and career when I almost gave up on my dream of building a successful marketing agency.

I had one of those moments when walking away from a ten-year-old business seemed more productive than pushing through the pain and continuing as an agency owner. I began spiralling down, over weeks of contemplation, lost in my own self-pity. Then I heard my father's voice say, 'When the going gets tough, the tough get going.' I heard the advice, 'If you want to get work, you've gotta pound the pavement.' I rose up with a renewed sense of determination and pride and I pounded the pavement.

I've lived a privileged life and for the majority of it my confidence and self-belief and drive were unquestionable. How did I go from being the luckiest and happiest bloke to becoming a downward spiralling business owner who let my self-talk convince me I was a failure and had no purpose?

My career story began growing up as one of the lucky Generation X. Because my mother had a computer for work, I was an early adopter of PC technology, which sparked my interest in computer-generated graphics, discovered via gaming.

I was one of forty graduates of the first ever Bachelor of Multimedia at Griffith University on the Gold Coast, Australia, and I began contracting as a multimedia freelancer at the beginning of my final year of university in 1998.

Over twenty years later and I've earned a few scars from failure, made a living from marketing successes, but above all I've learned a few things worth sharing, due to constantly trying to push the boundaries of my marketing skills and knowledge.

Local multimedia work was hard to come by after university. I was lucky enough to snag a contracting role, which was advertised on the university notice board. The company was called World Surfers Club and was way before its time, designing and developing Flash animated portals for pro-surfer diaries.

Flash was quite a novelty for multimedia web designers due to its ability to animate, but the file sizes it produced while most the world was still on dialup internet made for slow consumer adoption.

In 1998 on the Gold Coast, some businesspeople didn't even know what a website was. Selling my services was not all about digital – it was about adapting to the market conditions and educating people about the services I wanted to sell. They were innovative ones – they were exciting and they worked.

The Gold Coast wasn't ready to pay a multimedia producer to create websites, CD and DVD presentations. I got work elsewhere. In Brisbane, then Hong Kong, then the UK. The work was different but interesting and I got to be part of some great companies and their client contracts.

In Hong Kong, Invensys rail were working on recommissioning the Mass Transit Railways (MTR) SCADA system. My job was to break the software. Developers would give me their software and I would write a test document, execute it, break it – until it stopped breaking – and repeat. But the black and white Unix command line and Word documents weren't fulfilling my creative desires.

The Illusion Factor Design House in London did fulfil my creative desires, and in 2001 I had the pleasure of working on world-class brands while having the freedom to explore bigger ideas with bigger budgets. Graphic design, presentation design and Flash animation were mostly my bag, but when you're working on projects for British Telecom, Orange, Pirelli Tyres, Compaq and Jaguar you get to see behind the curtain and learn a lot about the inner workings of agencies and clients.

Back in Australia in 2001, I registered my first business name, MeMedia. I took several roles with Invensys, Body Science and RewardsCorp and on the side I helped my clients by designing and developing my own customised ecommerce shopping cart software and managed the content creation, search engine optimisation (SEO), adwords and social media marketing until 2006, when I decided to incorporate MeMedia as a company.

My dad always said, 'Don't let go of one rope until you've got hold of the other.' Without that client base, which was built on the side, I would not have had the confidence to start an agency. Because of those clients, I was working at almost full capacity straight out of the gates. There was finally a demand for my skills and creativity on the Gold Coast. The market had begun moving from innovation to early adoption of online shopping carts between 2001 and 2004.

I can't believe how much has changed since then and how much has stayed the same. I wish I hadn't made as many mistakes along the way, but still doing work for marketing clients who joined us as far back as 2004 shows me the risks we've taken were worth it.

MeMedia adapted with the market and is now better known as a content marketing agency that builds brands based on a methodology developed using the lessons I've learned throughout my career. We have been known as a web development agency, digital agency, marketing agency, integrated marketing agency, and our purpose has simply been to make our clients successful. In today's world, this is not enough; we discovered this while listening to market demand and adapting our methods.

In 2015, content marketing was all the hype but getting information on how to do this was hard. We commenced our own content marketing research and development project named Get Fact Up. This project was designed to test our theories around content marketing and develop a method we could then apply to our clients. We produced a video series, which focused on the latest trends in web design, development, social media and online advertising. We combined education, inspiration and entertainment with no agenda, just helpful information that businesses could easily understand and learn how they could take action.

In 2016, I was the first Gold Coaster awarded the title Community Digital Champion by the Queensland government for producing Get Fact Up. Since then, our content marketing method has been tested, broken, built back up, improved and adapted. This is the foundation that this book is built on. Years of challenges, failures and small successes all leading to a methodology that I can proudly say MeMedia lives and breathes and that our clients benefit from every day.

I've learned that marketing strategy is often put in the too hard/takes too long category or made too hard for marketers to understand and execute quickly and efficiently. I have tried, tested, broken, rebuilt and developed a strategic marketing framework that not only makes sense to the board and C-suite executives but also to the marketers who will execute it. The benefits of this approach serve all stakeholders and turn a place of work into a place where we all get to feel fulfilled. Where once a company was led by a CEO and a board of directors, now we must listen to an ever-changing marketplace and allow inspiration and influence to come from everywhere.

This strategic marketing framework is called PROACTIVE, and it has three important uses:

1. To develop your marketing strategy and question yourself, your team and your consumer market on what your purpose is, then to articulate how you will communicate and measure your marketing.

2. To plan your marketing campaigns via a one-page template to ensure all stakeholders are aware of the most important questions asked before and during a campaign.

3. To check your marketing activities against the framework and ensure your campaign was ACTIVE on everything you planned to do.

PROACTIVE PLANNER	CAMPAIGN	PERIOD
P Purpose	**R** Research	**O** Opportunity
A Audience	**C** Content	**T** Turn On
I Ignite	**V** Verification & Validation	**E** Evolve

The one-page PROACTIVE Planner

We will discuss the PROACTIVE framework in greater detail in Part Two of this book.

If you own, manage or work at a seven- to eight-figure business and have reached a plateau, are seeing a decrease in sales, are being overrun by competition or are experiencing internal cultural challenges, this book is for you. If you desire overnight success or the magic formula to record increased quarterly profits, this is not the book for you.

When I was a lot younger, impatient and seeking out tactics I could add to my marketing execution, books like this one seemed to be talking about ideas I just wasn't willing to adopt. I have always been obsessed with tactics. Obsessed with getting in and getting the job done. I've been able to spot an issue and simultaneously see a potential solution and start executing.

I'm grateful for having that 'get up and go' attitude and the willingness to be a solutionist, but this only gets you so far. Without strategy, without goals, without having a quick reference guide, a map and a compass, you're going to start veering off track. The more you keep your head down, executing, the more you're going to get lost in the wilderness. This is where the one-page PROACTIVE Planner stops marketers from chasing the shiny new idea and diving straight into execution and forces them to think strategically.

If you're adventurous but have grown up being more of a sprinter than a marathon runner, if you've always been quick to learn and quick to execute, if you have a knack for spotting the next big thing but haven't done anything about it, this book could help you too.

Rather than just being an observer of the concepts in this book, you can also partake in the exercises. I have included our methodology for creating your strategy and executing it, which I hope you get as much out of as my clients.

The internet changed the way people did business in the late 1990s. Running your business and adapting to a rapidly changing marketplace has been hard. Those who have adapted to changing markets, media and generational culture are my heroes. Despite their company size they've allowed their business to be market-led. They've been strategic and innovative but they are in the minority.

In recent years, world events have changed our daily lives, our future plans and what we value. Life doesn't get much more shocking than losing a loved one to bushfires or a virus, having to close your business or lose your job. With the realisation that maybe you won't be able to go about your life as you did before, dismay can easily consume you.

There was a time when I would have asked you to stop executing. Stop taking action for just a moment and sit and watch what is happening around you. Stop running on that treadmill, chasing greater success and profits. Get outside and see the world from a new angle and be strategic.

My hope is that you haven't been through a life-altering traumatic experience and that any turmoil you have experienced has been short lived or at worst has required you to think differently. Regardless of how your life and business have played out, you may have noticed a change in how people are feeling towards institutions and our lack of connection with businesses who put their profits as their purpose. It's been building for many years.

According to the World Health Organization (WHO), 'A lack of urgency, misinformation, and competing demands are blinding policy-makers from taking stock of a situation where mental disorders figure among the leading causes of disease and disability in the world.'[1]

Why is this? We haven't focused enough attention on what makes us happy. We are disconnected from our friends, family, ourselves, our community and our planet. But something has changed. If there is one thing we can thank the Covid-19 pandemic for, it's helping us to realise what's really important.

We have a fascination for and addiction to the internet, smartphones and social media, and the old-school marketing world with big advertising budgets tried to cash in. But many of us didn't want meaningless advertising to follow us from one device to another. Instead, we began craving education, entertainment, inspiration and emotional connection. We've become sensitised and empathetic and we as consumers are taking a stand.

It's taken worldwide events like global pollution killing wild animals, Brexit, riots in Hong Kong, climate change, a global pandemic and Black Lives Matter protests to make people feel they have a choice and a voice.

Hold onto your hats, company directors. If you fail to fix or define your company values, purpose beyond profit and your culture, you're not just going to feel the wrath of your customers. Your employees' productivity, absenteeism, retention and happiness are going to 'force' the suffering onto your bottom line, because the market has decided to choose liberty and happiness over dependence and dissatisfaction.

Recently the Australian Institute of Company Directors (AICD) released a handbook which considers the role of the board in leading their organisation towards ethically weighted 'should we?' questions. It's something I've been waiting for. With prestigious organisations such as the AICD endorsing this important change in our organisational needs, it brings me hope for cultural success.

Why is it needed? We've reached a tipping point. Can you feel it? A nostalgic 1960s-style 'power to the people' sentiment can be found all over the media. The tipping point for mass media attention was the UN Climate Action Summit held in New York on 23 September 2019.

As public protests ring out across the globe today, it's no wonder consumers feel disillusioned with governments and corporations. Consumers don't feel helpless. They feel empowered. While consumers are statistically blameless for planetary-scale threats requiring planetary-scale reforms, they are not helpless in influencing change for the betterment of society and the world.

Consumers and protesters have the tools and the power they need to not only disrupt daily commutes but also bring down organisations across the globe and create more ethical businesses in their place. Even if consumers don't exercise this level of frustration and technological sophistication, social media hashtags can do just the same, regardless of whether your company has a social profile or not.

While you may never have turned to social media to vent your frustrations at a poor customer experience, I would be surprised to hear that you haven't changed your consumption patterns or opinions of a brand in the hope corporations will change their production patterns, change their policies or enable more ethical competition into the market.

Proof that people were using their freedom of choice to make purchasing decisions made headlines in October 2019 when the Prime Minister of Australia, Scott Morrison, vowed to draft new laws to ban protesters from boycotting companies. The Human Rights Law Centre said the Prime Minister's announcement was another sign of an 'undemocratic trend' to undermine the right to protest, often 'at the behest' of big companies.[2]

Australia's 'liberal' government didn't seem so liberal anymore, and 'the people' were not going to take this lying down. We can't help it. It's in our DNA to want to be free and have freedom of choice.

The Australian bushfires of 2019 and 2020 were some of the worst on record:

> 'Thousands of firefighters and volunteers battled the fires, with millions of hectares burned, thousands of properties damaged, and countless numbers of wildlife exposed. In February 2020, the last fires were reportedly extinguished, with torrential rain assisting in putting out the remaining fires.'[3]

After almost two months of fires burning across Australia, the people had had enough. Australian comedian Celeste Barber had a large social media following. As she watched her family's house become engulfed in flames, Barber used Facebook's new donation feature to allow people to donate to the New South Wales rural fire service. While the government was still trying to work out how much and to whom they were going to provide funding, the world responded, with AUD

$51.3 million raised through Barber's record-breaking Facebook fundraiser.

Everyone has values that dictate their daily actions. They drive our mood, our motivation, who we love and especially who we give our hard-earned dollars to. We make purchasing decisions based on our values, often developed during our most formative years (before the age of eight), derived from the heroes we come to know and love throughout our lives.

According to UNICEF's work on measuring early childhood, which spans the period up to eight years of age, this time is critical for cognitive, social, emotional and physical development.[4] During these years, we develop values like empathy, respect, justice and hope. When we become teenagers, we want to feel part of a tribe that has similar values and beliefs and that makes us highly predictable creators and consumers.

Barber's bushfire fundraiser pulled together people with similar values. Charitable people from across the globe voted to make a change with their wallets, and felt relief that so many of their fellow human beings were cut from similar cloth.

The internet has empowered people to make significant change in the world. Change that is governed by our values and beliefs. We all know it's important to be on the right side of change; if your brand wishes to thrive beyond 2030, I suggest you build a brand on purpose, which in our language means building a PROACTIVE brand.

In this book I will provide examples of how founders and CEOs have leveraged their own personal values to guide an organisation's culture to improve the product they produce and better understand who they do it for.

PART ONE
VALUES AND PURPOSE

ONE

Why Is Culture So Important?

The origin of strategy

My experience in developing marketing strategies for clients forced me to ask the question, 'If the origin of strategy is culture, then what is the origin of culture?'. My research experience led me to understand that values inspire purpose, purpose inspires actions, actions inspire culture and, of course, culture is strategy.

Culture, purpose and values are often seen as buzz-words, but they're far from falling out of use, and for good reason. In his book, *This is Marketing*, Seth Godin says that 'culture is strategy' and breaks down what culture means: 'People like us do things like this.'[5] He's not just referring to employees – he's referring to friends, colleagues, associates and customers.

One definition of the word 'culture' from the Oxford English Dictionary is: 'the ideas, customs, and social behaviour of a particular person or society'.[6]

Before the internet, where did the biggest ideas spread? Religion. Religions have attracted and kept many believers and followers since time immemorial. According to the World Economic Forum:

> 'Christianity makes up 32.8% of the world's religions which makes it the largest religion on Earth. Christianity dominates in the Americas, Europe and the southern half of Africa and the rest of the world's religious beliefs are shared between Muslim 22.5%, Hindu 13.8%, Buddhist 7.2%, Atheist/Agnostic 11.8%, Jewish 0.2% and other 11.8%.'[7]

In Jordan Peterson's book, *12 Rules for Life*, he took some inspiration from religion:

'I couldn't understand how belief systems
could be so important to people that they were
willing to risk the destruction of the world
to protect them. I came to realise that shared
belief systems made them intelligible to one
another and that they weren't just about belief.'[8]

When people truly understand each other, they have empathy and feel a greater need to help those of similar beliefs. While beliefs and values are closely aligned, they are not the same. Our beliefs can and do change more regularly than our values. As we grow – physically, mentally and spiritually – we often come to understand that something we believed is no longer true.

Values inspire beliefs and I've found that our values rarely change, but that doesn't mean they can't or shouldn't. As John Demartini says, 'You don't need to blindly reject all of the values or social idealisms you were raised with. But neither can you simply assume that these values are necessarily your own.'[9]

My upbringing was privileged and predominantly positive. My relationship with my father was pure gold and, given his life success, I know that the majority of my values are not entirely my own. My belief has been that I simply need to follow in my father's footsteps to enjoy a similar life of success.

There is one value I hold dear that my father didn't quite share, which was health and nutrition. This became a point of frustration for me when my father was diagnosed with cancer and I wanted him to at least try consuming some of the herbal remedies that could have given him relief, and possibly a year or two more to live. His cancer was aggressive and incurable, but I shared his belief that he and his family might be able to enjoy more time. Unfortunately, his determination to do what was necessary dwindled rapidly as the cancer took over his body and mind.

I take inspiration from authors like Jordan Peterson, who says:

> 'The conditions of our lives become more and more personal and less and less comparable with those of others. Symbolically speaking, this means we must leave the house ruled by our father, and confront the chaos of our individual being. We must take note of our disarray, without completely abandoning that father in the process.'[10]

When we share values and purpose with other like-minded people, we can create a culture we're willing to stand for and protect.

My father's death made me reject the faith I once put in the medical system as their only form of prescribed treatment was chemotherapy. They did nothing to educate my father on nutritional support he could have implemented. His blind respect for doctors' advice also meant that unless they said it, it probably wasn't true. I have a passion for research and often enjoy learning about nutrition, and find myself relishing any discussion on this topic – even if it's a debate with the GP.

I am not religious but the majority of my father's values stemmed from religion. Clearly, it's possible to have similar values but not the same beliefs.

How might our values influence the services we deliver or the products we make?

Many founders and marketers of brands have figured out that building a brand on purpose and values, then manufacturing products or producing services based on these, can bring you closer to your customer.

The founders of Patagonia, Yvon Chouinard and Vincent Stanley, published *The Responsible Company* in 2012.[11] Patagonia, a gear and clothing retailer, is often held up as proof that it's possible to have an environmentalist approach to business and still be financially successful.

Yvon Chouinard was originally an adventurer, rock climber, surfer, kayaker and falconer. In 1957, he taught himself blacksmithing, bought a second-hand coal-fired forge, and started making hardened steel pitons and eventually started Chouinard Equipment. Patagonia was founded in 1973. Always a lover of nature, Chouinard couldn't help but influence Patagonia's product line, the first of which was his hardened steel pitons for use in climbing in the Yosemite Valley.

By 1970, Chouinard Equipment was the biggest supplier of climbing hardware in the US, but the pitons (climbing spikes) they produced damaged rockfaces. They wanted to move towards a more environmentally friendly option and invented 'aluminium chocks that could be wedged by hand rather than hammered in and out of cracks... Within a few months of the catalog's mailing, the piton business had atrophied; chocks sold faster than they could be made.'[12]

Changing climbing products was only the first sign that Patagonia could live their personal values through their business and Chouinard later committed the company to using all organic cotton. This came with a price. Early in the release of their new organic cotton clothing range, Patagonia experienced a consumer adjustment period to their increased pricing on garments. They stayed true to their product line, their values and their purpose and it wasn't long before their organic range began taking off. In 2002, Yvon Chouinard founded 1% for the Planet, and Patagonia became the first business to commit 1% of annual sales to the environment.

In 2020, the 1% for the Planet network consists of over 3,000 businesses and individuals that contribute to environmental non-profits in over ninety countries. To date, 1% for the Planet has directed over $250 million to these grassroots organisations working toward a better world. [13]

But why? Naysayers believe donating 1% to charity and having a philanthropic purpose is a business killer, a distraction and does nothing to support the success of a business. Yvon Chouinard bucked that trend and there are many more like him and Patagonia. Chouinard's environmentalist values have steered Patagonia for almost fifty years and still guide them today. Their customers are those who value the environment; they climb and are grateful for Patagonia's supply of products, which enable them to leave their favourite climbing wall intact.

Climbing has a culture of its own and, because Chouinard was part of that culture, he understood the problems they faced. His entrepreneurial spirit was what helped him to solve those problems. His values meant that he solved them not only for the climber but also for the planet. His ties to his values were strengthened when he realised that the climbing community appreciated his way of doing business and supported Patagonia by voting with their wallets.

Acknowledging values and culture in your organisation

Acknowledgement by such organisations as the AICD marks a significant milestone in corporate adoption of the importance of culture in our organisations, but few understand where to start. General Stanley McChrystal says in his book *Team of Teams* that: 'Order can emerge from the bottom up, as opposed to being directed with a plan, from the top down.'[14]

The building of corporate culture requires open-mindedness and an inclusive approach, involving key stakeholders from each department of your corporation.

Tim Cook was named the new CEO of Apple on 24 August 2011 and most within the organisation didn't believe he was the right person for the job. Apple's founder, Steve Jobs, was known as a visionary and someone who would stop at nothing to produce the best products.

Cook focused upon building a harmonious culture that meant 'weeding out people with disagreeable person-alities – people Jobs tolerated and even held close'.[15] He made headlines when he challenged shareholders to 'get out of the stock' if they didn't share the company's views on sustainability and climate change.

Leander Kahney writes:

'Cook believes strongly that companies should have a good strategy coupled with good values. In late 2017, his six core values for running Apple were quietly published in an obscure financial statement, and subsequently were given their own subsections on Apple's website.'[16]

While Cook holds the values close, he has ensured that order can emerge from the bottom up by sharing these common values with Apple's employees. In a 2019 interview, Cook explained how many of the issues of the environment, privacy, education and immigration are personal for Apple's employees and said, 'I would hope that every CEO would stand up and represent their employees.'[17]

If we wish to create a culture that respects and empowers each employee to be passionate about the work they do, leaders must lead by discovering what the shared values are. Leaders must become champions for shared values by setting and keeping standards that are not compromised.

Cultural change is hard, but when you make the necessary effort to operate by your values, those who disagree will leave and those who are on board will stay. In the end, you'll find yourself with a team that works well together, finds solutions to problems without your input and always has both the company's and the customers' best interests at heart.

I know this from my personal experience and from the extensive research I have done. I am far from perfect but, because I've had an open mind and a willingness to change for the better, I've consistently improved the culture of my own business and kept long-term employees. My own personal values have brought me here and they are going to propel me forward.

TWO

Discovering Your Purpose

Knowing your purpose is fundamental to not only delivering positive marketing outcomes but also for directing companies, building a great company culture and inspiring your crew, customers and community.

Why do we need a purpose?

Culture, values, purpose – pick up any marketing text written in the last decade and you'll likely be bombarded with these terms. These words are far more than a 21st-century buzzword kit designed to make entrepreneurs feel better about themselves and their actions.

Understood correctly and implemented into your business model, values, purpose and culture can make a positive impact on the strategic direction of your business or organisation.

Today's consumers are disillusioned with the corporate sector and, given the growing number of ignoble – and painfully public – mistakes by profit-as-purpose companies, who can blame them? There's little trust anymore, thanks to 'fake news', and faceless, money-hungry corporations around the world have done little to change the public's less than glowing opinion.

Consumers have reached their threshold, and something has to change. If a business has any hope of achieving longevity in today's saturated market, it's imperative to establish a trusting relationship with the market by adopting an authentic purpose.

In 2016, PricewaterhouseCoopers (PwC) conducted a survey which showed that 79% of business leaders believe an organisation's purpose is central to business success.[18]

In 2018, Cone and Porter Novelli surveyed more than 1,000 Americans on their attitudes about purpose-driven companies, which revealed that 80% of consumers say they're more loyal to purpose-driven brands.[19]

For organisations to become purpose-led, they need to solve a real-world problem by providing a product which is created by adhering to a clearly identified set of company values and a purpose statement. A purpose states how you plan to be of service and allows customers to understand how you fit with their set of values and how you plan to do good within the business ecosystem.

Simon Sinek has written that 'why' is a more important decision-swaying factor than 'what'. In his 2019 book, *The Infinite Game*, he goes deeper, explaining that businesses need a just cause – 'something bigger than themselves or the company'.

Sinek argues that the game of business is not bound by a finite set of rules:

> 'Companies exist to advance something –
> technology, quality of life or anything else
> with the potential to ease or enhance our lives
> in some way, shape or form. That people are
> willing to pay money for whatever a company
> has to offer is simply proof that they perceive
> or derive some value from those things.'[20]

To define their purpose, businesses need to know who they are, who they serve and what problem they solve. Answer these questions and you're on your way to building a business with staying power. Ignore them and you're only setting yourself up to be forgotten.

Companies that solely focus on generating profit run the risk of alienating themselves from the modern marketplace. Why? Because they give nothing back. They have no culture, no values and no purpose beyond dollar signs.

If this is the first time you've delved into purpose as a way to understand and redefine your personal (and your brand's) reason for existing, rest assured this conversation has been going on for some time.

One of the earliest western influencers on this topic was Ralph Waldo Emerson, the American philosopher, poet and essayist. 'Self-reliance', an essay written in 1841, contained one of his recurrent themes: the need for each individual to avoid conformity and false consistency, and follow his own instincts and ideas. Emerson emphasises the importance of individualism and its effect on an individual's satisfaction in life. He stresses that anyone is capable of achieving happiness if they simply change their mindset. Emerson focuses on seemingly insignificant details explaining how life is 'learning and forgetting and learning again'.[21]

Being open-minded and accepting of intelligent criticism is important, but until we reach a level of emotional intelligence, it's hard for us to distinguish what is real and what is fake. Given the age of information and smart devices we live in, emotion is rarely felt through text and the distance enforced by electronic devices.

As I watch my teenage daughters go through the trials and tribulations of finding their tribe and seeking social acceptance, I feel their pain. Given my fascination with psychology, consumer behaviour and how humans interact, I can't help but feel a little disdain for social media. Just because we have the ability to communicate our every thought and feeling via text, it doesn't mean we should. While technology has given us great opportunities to be 'connected' and 'find our purpose', many people seem more lost than ever. If you're having a crisis of confidence and you don't know where your life is leading or what your purpose is, you're not alone.

If you're around the age of twenty-five, it's quite possible you're having a quarter-life crisis. I had one and that's when I chose to travel the world. Your purpose is to be young and as free as you can be, to live life and be adventurous. Take life as it comes, see new things, explore new places, new ideas, make mistakes and have as many new experiences as your heart desires.

If you're an ambitious high achiever and aspire to be a billionaire by the time you're thirty, this advice may not sit well with you. It's entirely possible your purpose already exists because you've discovered – earlier than most – that your purpose is to be of service to others and you've discovered a problem worth solving.

While social media has driven a wedge between many, it has brought others together, especially when it comes to helping people, animals or the Earth. The bushfires response discussed earlier is a good example of this, as the *New York Times* noted in its coverage:

> '"This is a seminal moment in Australia when it comes to philanthropy and giving," said Krystian Seibert, a fellow at the Center for Social Impact at Swinburne University of Technology in Melbourne. "I haven't seen something like it before."'[22]

We can attribute this kind of global outpouring of generosity to the power of social media and the people on it. Of course, the majority of humans hate seeing people and animals in pain, but the notion that giving can make us feel good – even happy – can be foreign.

People behave altruistically when they see others in desperate circumstances and feel empathy and a desire to help. We can thank our own neuroscience for this. The brain is remarkable and complex, but the neurochemical drivers of happiness are quite easy to identify. Dopamine, serotonin and oxytocin make up what is called the 'happiness trifecta'. Any activity that increases the production of these neurochemicals will cause a boost in mood.

Oxytocin is at the top of the list of hormones we want pumping through our veins. Not only does it boost our mood, it also helps to counteract cortisol, the stress hormone. Oxytocin also doesn't like to work alone, as it has been proven to also increase serotonin and dopamine. Serotonin helps improve sleep, learning, digestion, appetite and memory. Dopamine is connected to motivation and arousal.[23]

When we are being of service to others, considerate of their well-being and spend time or money showing it, we're being altruistic. Altruism leads to the production of Oxytocin, an improved mood and a sense of happiness. Having a purpose beyond (but not in place of) profit will help motivate you and your team, and will breed a happy company culture.

Once you acknowledge and share your values and purpose within your company, not only will your internal brand build but your external marketing will exhibit the tone, happiness and empathy which will inspire your customers to want to do business with you.

Knowing your personal purpose

Just like when you're receiving instructions from airline stewards about what to do in case of an emergency, take care of yourself first then take care of others. Discover your personal values and purpose first and then we can care for our team.

I've discussed the topic of 'knowing your personal purpose' with hundreds of people and it's astounding how many are unable to answer this question but have a desire to know their purpose. Maybe they've never thought about it, but the reason we're having this conversation is because while getting to know them, I've found they are feeling lost.

That word – lost. It scares a lot of us. It's the feeling of not knowing where you are, which way is north, where your friends and family are, whether you have enough 'fuel' to get where you're going and even how you might obtain that 'fuel'. What is our life purpose? Are we really supposed to know?

If we try too hard to nail it down and define it, could we be missing out on discovering or impacting something bigger than ourselves or the specific purpose we seek? Isn't it only natural we question ourselves and our purpose? Isn't it only natural that when we are surrounded by amazing human beings, their ambitions become our altruistic dreams? Why have we become so impatient? Has instant access to sensory pleasure rewired our brains to become addicted to the dopamine reward system?

Music, movies, podcasts, books, buy now pay later, alcohol, drugs and companionship on call has us addicted, impatient and seeking instant reward. This instantly rewarding world has made us forget we need to be of service for the long term. The saying 'All good things come to those who wait' is incomprehensible to most.

We need to solve bigger problems than those that give instant reward. We need to not be addicted. We need to take time out. Breathe. Sit in silence and think of those who are grateful for our existence because of the unique powers that we hold and our willingness to express them. Without judgement and in the only way we know how.

Our personal purpose cannot be defined by singular passions. We are passionate people and, because we are lucky enough to live in a world where we can find freedom, we can record our dreams to live a life which fills us with energy. At times, we feel like we could power the sun. The problem is that we dream too little or too large and rarely in between.

Our forefathers have left some amazing legacies, but did they really know what legacy they were going to leave while they were first embarking on their journey? Would they have described their personal and brand purpose as a singular discovery, product or brand?

Steve Jobs is described as a visionary – someone who believed that people deserved artistic, intuitive, powerful but simple technology which enabled even greater creativity, privacy and security. Walter Isaacson wrote in his biography of Steve Jobs that upon Steve's death, 'It was refreshing to see an entrepreneur celebrated. He may have been a billionaire businessman, but he became so by crafting beautiful products that made lives more magical.'[24]

Jobs got lost, too. You think visionaries don't go off on tangents and make mistakes? His company NeXT was full of self-centred ego, but if it wasn't for that little detour, Apple and Pixar might never have survived.

According to Isaacson, Jobs knew he was going to live a short life and so he was naturally impatient. It served Apple and Pixar well, but plenty would say he didn't go about it very nicely. His impatience was applied in a constructive way. Instead of consuming, he created and iterated and created again and would not ship until each product was perfect. He had a great purpose, and I suspect he didn't spend time worrying about how it would be seen or what his legacy would be – he just got on with it.

My hope is that you don't get so bogged down in perfection that you have paralysis by analysis. Prolific is better than perfect. Try personal purposes on and see how they fit. You might like many. One for each day of the week and each moment of the day. Those that work for you at each given moment are perfect because they allowed you to be in the moment and move forward.

If thinking too big gives you anxiety, that's completely natural and maybe a planetary purpose is not for you. Being over ambitious can cause anxiety, but if you've got this far I'm guessing you're a visionary who wants to make a bigger impact than just your own back pocket, and that means thinking big.

One way to make it feel a little more achievable is to scale it back a bit or change the time frame. Find a middle ground. We all fit somewhere, for we are part of a complex and diverse ecosystem. A modern-day wilderness full of adventure and excitement and some downright difficult challenges.

Not all of us should be trying to 'save the world'. Focus on a local problem first. Maybe it's local to you or somewhere else but be a little more specific in your personal purpose. Knowing where we've come from is exactly where we need to be to start to understand ourselves and find the values that define us. These values are the clues to finding your purpose.

THREE

Discovering Your Values

I was nearly forty and I was having the stereotypical midlife crisis but without the affair, divorce and sports cars. I was comparing myself with others and the expectation that I should be successful. I was trying to be 'present' in two businesses and while there were fun times being had, I didn't feel I was on track to achieving my work and life goals. I was grumpy, mildly depressed, frustrated and lost.

Leigh Kelson and I co-founded an entrepreneurial 'edutainment' business, BeachCity Media (BCM), which produced over 3,000 live video productions between 2015 and 2020. Leigh is a serial entrepreneur and far more experienced in building and exiting businesses. BCM was playing second fiddle to my marketing agency, MeMedia, and for me to be part of BCM, this wasn't going to work. MeMedia still needed me, and Leigh knew this. He said, 'Chris, if you want to ride two horses you need two arses and I don't know anyone with two arses.' I stepped back from BCM.

MeMedia had some great key people in it but because I wasn't championing the brand so much as I was being the 'anchor man' for BCM, MeMedia began to struggle. My feeling of disappointment in myself was overwhelming. How could I let this happen? The thought of shutting down was too much to bear and came with a raft of emotions. At this point of failure I knew something had to change both within myself and my business, but discovering what was something I felt the need to work out on my own.

I thought about my father's values and how hard he worked. He took over his parents' farm and lived out his dream of running a cattle farm, and started a business using the property as a base to transport the local farmers' produce to market. I spent a lot of weekends and school holidays with my dad, and in between loading pallets of avocados for market, we would be fixing fences, irrigation pipes and tractors, and building cattle yards and gates.

The property had around sixteen acres of grass and with a maximum of thirteen cattle, we knew all of them by name. They were more pets than produce, and I never thought of them any other way during those years. My dad and I got emotionally attached, especially to one bull, Marvel, who was rejected by his mother due to a traumatic birth and so we had to hand rear him. He eventually grew into a huge animal that I knew well and treated as if he was a small pet.

Learning to become a farmer meant that interaction with other farmers was a highly valuable experience and the cattle sales were where all the action took place. My dad was never shy about introducing himself to fellow cattlemen who he'd never met. With a slow walk up to the yards, half leaning on the gates, he'd extend his hand and say, 'G'day, Geoff Hogan from Tamborine Mountain. How ya goin'?'

When I was struggling to regain my motivation and understand my purpose, it was these stories I started to reflect on, and they helped me greatly. I had finally discovered the reason for my failure and it felt as though my biggest life challenge was meant to be, because it was where I found one of my biggest breakthroughs in both life and business.

I found my own values by remembering these childhood moments and recognising the values my father had. He grew up in a traditional farmer's home and so he valued hard work, nature, providing for and protecting his family. When I thought about this, I realised I'm just a chip off the old block, with a few tweaks from my own life experiences. I was also inspired by

Eckhart Tolle's book, *A New Earth*.[25] The combination of these realisations helped me develop a way to work out not only my own personal values and purpose but others' too.

By trying and testing this value-finding method with friends, family, clients and team members, I realised that just because my father was my inspiration, that doesn't mean their fathers were. We can have multiple people in our lives whose personality traits, morality, work ethic or romantic nature we admire. The key here is that you feel you know them intimately. That you can identify with their values. As Steve Jobs said: 'One way to remember who you are is to remember who your heroes are.'[26]

In 1997, when Jobs returned to Apple, he wanted to revitalise the Apple brand by creating a 'brand image campaign, not a set of advertisements featuring products'. He wanted to sign Lee Clow, the creative director of Chiat/Day – the same agency that had created the 1984 ad for the launch of Macintosh, which was a huge success.

Jobs and Clow created the well-known 'Think Different' campaign, which celebrated 'the crazy ones. The misfits. The rebels. The troublemakers. The round pegs in square holes. The ones who see things differently'. It went on to explain that 'while some may see them as the crazy ones, we see genius. Because the people who are crazy enough to think they can change the world are the ones who do'.

As Jobs pointed out, the campaign was launched not just at customers but at the people who made up the Apple company: 'We at Apple had forgotten who we were. One way to remember who you are is to remember who your heroes are. That was the genesis of that campaign.'[27]

Whoever your heroes are – a family member, teacher, sports coach, sensei, mentor or celebrity – discovering and analysing what you think their values are is easier than starting from scratch and trying to think of your own.

I offer my personal story to help you see that there may be many people in your life from as far back as you can remember who can help you discover your values, which influence your personal purpose and ultimately your brand purpose. Remembering their quotes and knowing their values can be valuable, especially on those days when you need to pick yourself up from a tough confrontation.

Once you've discovered your values, you'll begin to realise that everyone has values which dictate their daily actions, whether they're conscious of it or not. They can drive our mood, our motivation, who we love and especially who we give our time and hard-earned dollars to. If our values dictate so much of our lives and consumer behaviour, it's imperative that we know not only our own but also those around us, and in business that means your team and your customers.

Our goal in marketing and advertising is to emotionally connect with our audience. People remember how you make them feel, and those who engage with you or your marketing emotionally will never forget you. Emotions last long after the first engagement and if emotion is attached to the purchase, the feeling also lasts.

Be wary of what values and emotions you attach to your brand. They must be personal to be authentic. No matter what your story is, when you embrace the values and lessons you've learned from them, your passion for your brand will be stronger.

Finding your values

Writing down your values during this time of reflection is important but turning feelings into words can be challenging. If you struggle with this, as most people do, let's start with finding out who you admired when you were growing up and what you think their values were. If you can't name anybody from your youth, try to think of a celebrity or sports person.

David Attenborough is one of my heroes. His life's work is admirable and his 2020 documentary *A Life on Our Planet* reflects on his first-hand accounts of humanity's impact on Earth.[28] This documentary was scientifically revealing and explained, in layman's terms, how we can right our wrongs and the consequences if we don't.

Without knowing him personally, I have spent enough time watching his documentaries that I believe I could describe his values. Bravery, humility, charity, community, empathy, accountability, honesty, adventurousness, trustworthiness, inquisitiveness, freedom, boldness, creativity, curiosity, happiness, leadership, doing meaningful work and peace are all values I would associate with David Attenborough.

Every time I do this with somebody, they are astounded that they possess almost all the same values as their idol. We want to be like those we admire. We would almost trade lives but instead we'll do our best to live out these values in our own life, which becomes a self-inspiring belief and one worth remembering.

John Demartini describes the process of discovering your values as filling a void: 'Whatever we perceive is missing [from our life] sets off a powerful hunger for precisely that thing. The perception of lack or void creates a corresponding value that drives us until we feel fulfilled.'[29]

I have taken on a lot of my father's values but, when I disagreed with his, I established my own. When he was young, he was athletic and valued that. When he became a father, that became less important, and with the social acceptance of pie eating and beer drinking it was normal to be carrying a few extra kilos. When I was young, I was determined never to have a belly, although this requires a lot of discipline. Health and fitness are high on my list of values.

Similarly, while I enjoyed caring for and raising cattle as a cattle farmer's son, I didn't so much enjoy what happened to them after they left the farm. One year after my father died, I became vegan and now follow a plant-based diet. I discovered that I valued my love of nature more than destruction and therefore meat was no longer on the menu.

If you do an internet search for 'list of values', you'll find helpful lists of up to 200 core values. Take these, print them out and start underlining those your hero possesses. Then tick those you share.

When I have done this exercise, my list looks something like this:

- Accountability
- Bravery
- Creativity
- Charity
- Community
- Courage

- Discipline
- Empathy
- Energy
- Family
- Freedom
- Gratitude
- Honesty

- Inquisitiveness
- Integrity
- Leadership
- Respect
- Transparency
- Trustworthiness
- Vitality

The ones I could not live my life without are:

- Family
- Freedom
- Adventure
- Vitality
- Honesty

- Creativity
- Bravery
- Empathy
- Respect

Taking these values, trace them back to who impressed them upon you and what moments they relate to. In those moments, you will be able to discover more about yourself and this is where the storytelling begins.

I remember feeling empathy towards someone's needs when my eldest sister and I were walking through Brisbane. We had just passed several homeless people on the street and after walking past the fifth one I stopped my sister, went back and gave them my only

20 cents. I was around seven at the time and my sister told me that I was a generous and loving person and she was proud of me. Since that day, my empathetic values have helped me remain charitable, be better at listening and making friends and being good at understanding customers' needs. All of these things bring me joy.

Take the time to write down a story which describes a time when you first discovered your values, how you felt and times when you have lived out these values in later life. Actions always speak louder than words so you will soon find that if you haven't lived out these values, maybe they're not ingrained in who you are, but possibly more who you desire to become.

How your values describe your purpose

In the previous exercise, you may have found and tested some of your beliefs on what your values are compared to whether you live out those values. This inherently helps define your purpose.

My main purpose is to protect and provide food and a home for my family. This is why I get out of bed every morning, go to work and earn a living.

My secondary purpose is to make memorable moments with my wife and three girls. This is why I work damn hard to make my clients happy so I can grow my business and take my kids on holidays.

My third purpose is to be adventurous, courageous and prepared. Staying fit and healthy by exercising, hiking, surfing and performing martial arts are the activities and habits I've formed to keep me aligned to this purpose.

What do I have to do at work to ensure I'm delivering on these personal promises? Being a marketing director, I have to be a creative problem solver, which requires me to empathise with my client and their customers, to be able to see how people want their business to show up for the customers and their team.

Sometimes I fall victim to being over-empathetic, which makes me feel the pain and suffering our potential clients might be going through. Being of a protective nature, I want to save them. I've learned to manage this and, rather than absorb pain and suffering, let it wash over me like a wave, but that doesn't mean I ignore my emotions – I just harness them to aid my work.

By going through this process, I have discovered I am fortunate to be in my position as a marketer. I can be of service to many people in creative ways and this makes my work fulfilling because my business is a vehicle for my values and purpose.

In a single day, my purpose can change from being a film director to a marketing strategist, art director, course creator, presenter, salesperson and leader. I'm fortunate that these activities are possible in my line of work, which is why I think I'm so happy here.

For most people, the same level of happiness in your work is possible. This exercise enables you to find the good in any career or position. As long as you have a great workplace culture, room for personal growth and a sense of freedom with your work, you can find happiness in anything you do.

Can you fill in the blanks in the statements below?

Personal purpose statement

I go to work so that I may support my [self/ family]............to have............

I am a [insert at least three of your values]............person who enjoys expressing my [insert another three of your values]............values at work, which enables me to produce/be the best [insert work functions or activities]............for my............[team/managers/clients].

I feel most valued when I receive............from my............

I feel most supported at work when............

I feel............when our customers say............

FOUR

Adapting Your Personal Purpose To A Brand Purpose

As Stanley McChrystal says: 'Purpose affirms trust, trust affirms purpose.'[30] As with your personal purpose, and learning what values resonate within you, the same understanding needs to be developed with the market you serve and your team. It's time to take your team on the same journey of discovery via a workshop. This may seem like a daunting task, but bear with me.

Businesses of all sizes have departments with a figure-head or key stakeholder who acts as the glue which binds the department and others together. Some of these people are the glue by title only and others are the glue because they truly care about their teammates.

Both types of people are important in gaining feedback, but having all of them in a workshop is hard to accomplish. By choosing around ten of these people, you will embark on getting to know their personal values and their personal purpose.

To help you choose the group of representatives, start with a company-wide SWOT analysis. If your company has never done an internal SWOT (strengths, weaknesses, opportunities and threats) check, hold onto your hats. The first time is often the hardest.

After distributing a document to your entire team, allow up to one week for them to complete and return the SWOT to you. People can remain anonymous but sometimes this inhibits your ability to understand the underlying reasons why they may have provided a specific answer. Instead, I inform everybody of this and emphasise that while we want people to feel free to share their concerns, we would prefer them to share them openly, honestly and without fear of repercussion. This way you will be able to gather more data if need be.

Providing a way for all employees to give their viewpoint on the organisation's strengths, weaknesses, opportunities and threats not only helps build trust within an organisation, it also creates an opportunity to see things from multiple perspectives.

Analysing this data and distilling it down to the most important themes under each heading will assist in developing insight into the most pertinent topics.

Internal values workshop

As Simon Sinek says, 'People don't buy what you do, they buy why you do it.'[31] Values and beliefs are the why, but many of us have forgotten why we do anything except to make money and provide for our family.

Starting with each individual's personal journey, directors, managers and employees are able to rediscover themselves and their values. These help us articulate our purpose and who we want to work with, both internally and externally (suppliers, distributors and consumers).

A breakthrough moment is when we discover that these personal values are actually our commercial values. This is achieved when, working with several different combinations of value structures, we define a purpose story – then it's time to test.

Conducting this workshop can take anywhere from a half day to a full day, depending on how much you want people to share or some of the emotional stories which may be released. The stories are where the gold lies and should not be hindered, apart from a general rule on time allowed for sharing. The stories should be encouraged and not criticised. Use the opportunity to note keywords from them to reveal the actions people take in their daily lives when they live out their values.

Before you start this workshop with your team, there are a few rules:

1. Describe the goal of the day before you invite people.

    – 'To discover our corporate purpose by embarking on a journey of personal discovery.'

    – 'Our intention is to unite the company and nurture a company culture we are all proud to be part of.'

2. Allow the entire organisation to be part of the day.

    – 'All people within the company will have a chance to share their point of view via an anonymous internal company SWOT.'

    – Allow those invited to refuse to be part of the one-day workshop.

3. Be clear about the rules of the day.

    – 'Everything that is divulged in the safe space where your workshop is held is 100% confidential and your thoughts and feelings can be expressed without repercussion.'

4. Allow people to leave if they feel uncomfortable sharing in front of others.

5. Have everybody acknowledge that these rules have been shared.

6. At the end of the workshop, you may express that should they wish to place their name at the top of the first page, this may help with any questions the workshop facilitators have with clarifying their words and feelings.

7. No personal details on the forms will be shared unless it is approved by you and by the CEO/ management in the final documentation.

Know the market

If you've come to know your internal team's values, it's important to understand your customer. If you conduct an existing business, invite your ideal customers to the table. Serve coffee and come to understand their pain points and their values. Be open. Have a laugh. Enjoy this time together. It's important to know how you can best be of service by understanding exactly who your customers are.

The more customers, the better the data. If you're a small company with only a few customers, do your best to ask all of them and maybe let them suggest other companies they think you should work with and then ask for a coffee date or quick phone call. If having customers in the room doesn't work, hit the phones or video chat with them. It's not as powerful but will still be effective.

Once you have a base of understanding the common problems your ideal customer has in relation to your business, you can determine how you best solve the problem.

If you don't feel you have enough data, conducting a poll on LinkedIn or Facebook is most likely the easiest way to determine which problems are shared most with people in your network. If those people in your network are nothing like your ideal customer, an email survey might be another way you can boost your numbers. You can create surveys in numerous web software applications and these can be sent as links to your social media contacts.

People whose opinion is valued often don't mind being part of a survey because they like to see how they compare to their peers. Make sure you explain that their opinion is valued because of their status or experience.

Serving the customer vs serving the team

I'm often asked if we put our team or our customers first and how this impacts our brand values and purpose.

This is where a lot of organisations get confused. It's important to remember that if we didn't solve a customer's problem, we wouldn't have a business. In terms of our purpose, it's the customer first.

We align our actions, quality of work, customer service, presentation and style via core brand values. By solving the customer's problem in our own unique, value-driven way, this is how we differentiate ourselves from our competitors and stay authentic.

This allows us to remain consistent in how and what we are prepared to do to solve our customers' problem(s). Our brand values help protect us from feeling 'unhappy' about the work we produce or the style of service we provide because we didn't compromise on our values.

Your brand is not a CSR programme

Your brand's purpose should not be a corporate social responsibility (CSR) programme designed to put your charitable organisation, volunteering or ethically oriented practices before your customers' problems. These can often be the result of operating a profitable organisation.

The reason CSR programmes are considered 'old hat' is that they often don't benefit your customer first and focus too heavily on the community and social benefit. They are easily brushed off by customers due to the lack of alignment to a particular charitable cause or planetary problem. Not seeing eye to eye with a customer on certain beliefs – such as whether climate change is real or not – shouldn't prevent you from doing business with them. A brand's purpose is only a potential barrier to purchase when the CSR is the first reason for your existence.

This does not mean being charitable should not be part of your profit distribution. It just means that you need to put your consumers' buying considerations and benefits first. Some brands feel incomplete without a CSR. Many product-based brands base their entire manufacturing and material supply on ethical and sustainable practices and I'm all for it, so long as the benefit to the customer is prioritised.

Zambrero's is an Australian Mexican franchise that creates nutritious and healthy fast food and contributes to charitable causes. My primary reason for purchasing from Zambrero's is that it's healthy and, when I've completed my transaction, the feeling which lasts longer than the taste of a beautiful burrito is the knowledge that I also helped feed somebody in a third-world country.

Zero Co Australia exist solely to 'win the war on waste at your place'. They do this by 'delivering incredible personal-care and home-cleaning products direct to your door (minus all the single use plastic)'. It looks as though Zero Co's purpose is leading with a CSR but because they deliver their products, provide simple reply-paid methods to help with the refill, reduce the 'waste at your place' and help reduce landfill, they are blurring the lines but in a compelling way.

To get a first-hand experience of the importance of putting the customer at the forefront of your purpose, I recently interviewed Harvee Pene, TEDx speaker and co-author of *Cashed Up*.[32]

Cashed Up explains seven steps to gain more money, time and happiness from your business, which is based on him joining forces with Ben Walker to lead the award-winning team of life-changing accountants at Inspire. Harvee spent five years transforming Inspire from a cash-building good idea to a seven-figure impact machine, recognised as one of the top 100 companies in Australia. Harvee said:

'Inspire became really well known for the giving initiative called Day for Dollar, where for every dollar of tax that we practically saved our small business clients, we gave a day of access to food, water, health and sanitation to families in need.'

While Inspire have become well known for charitable giving, their loyalty first and foremost is to their customer and, in April 2016, Inspire launched the Save 500,000 Tax Campaign to help clients save tax, giving proactive advice and helping people make smart financial decisions before the end of the financial year.

'It was mission impossible. We thought, by our own calculations, we might hit $100,000 or $200,000 in tax savings, but we blew our own expectations in twelve weeks, we ended up saving our clients $1.26 million, which was an incredible feat.'

In their first campaign, Inspire were not only able to save their customers money, but they were also able to donate over one million days of food, water and health sanitation to families. Inspire's customers clearly came because they wanted to save money but the feeling of helping someone other than themselves lasted long after the transaction with Inspire. This charitable drive became the successful Day for Dollar initiative.

PART TWO
PROACTIVE MARKETING

PRO ACT IVE

The PROACTIVE Marketing Methodology

Being able to say that our strategic marketing methodology works every time we implement it makes me proud of my team and our journey. We've tried so hard to break this model and, if we hadn't, I know I wouldn't be writing this book.

By breaking it, I mean removing some of the steps in our methodology due to client pressure to cut corners, or reducing our marketing retainer, or simply thinking, 'We don't need to do that part this month.' We were able to see that the results were not as quick or as solid when the methodology wasn't implemented in its entirety.

These are the components of the PROACTIVE Marketing Method:

- Purpose

- Research

- Opportunity

- Audience

- Content

- Turn On

- Ignite

- Validation

- Evolve

Consistency is key and if this model isn't repeated month after month, prepare not to see results. When should you start seeing results? It depends on your volume and how often you hit people's eyeballs, gather data and engage with them emotionally. The first question I normally get after discussing this with clients is: how long does it take for somebody to buy?

The earliest marketing advice that gives an actual number dates back to 1885, in a book called *Successful Advertising* by Thomas Smith.[33]

According to Smith, it takes a potential customer to see your advertisement twenty times before they will buy. Does this mean that if somebody saw my ad every day for twenty days I could expect them to purchase inside the month? Unfortunately, that's not my experience, but the principle is still valid.

A more recent study with some science behind it is Google's Zero Moment of Truth (ZMOT) study from 2011, which refers to how a consumer behaves before they take action to make a purchase.[34] Google's study uncovered that most people don't buy the first time they come into contact with you, your product or your service. Google found that buyers need seven hours of interaction with your brand across eleven touch points in four different locations.

For example, if you meet somebody for a coffee or they come into your store to browse your range and they spend fifteen minutes with you, you've still got six hours and forty-five minutes of time to spend with them before they'll buy. Doing this with every customer isn't possible, especially if you had to meet them eleven times across four different locations. The production of marketing assets gives you the ability to spend more time with your potential customer, whether at home, at work, via social media, blogs, your website and so on.

In my 2015–2016 live research study for content marketing, named Get Fact Up, we released educational, entertaining and inspirational video content every week for fifty-eight weeks. We distributed them via social media and email marketing and hosted the show on YouTube and on our own website.

At around the sixteenth episode – four months into the show – our Google rankings started to hit the first page of Google, the phone started to ring and enquiries began trickling in, all attributed to Get Fact Up. By the end of fifty episodes, we had experienced an increase of 20% in new sales for the year, and had achieved the following successes:

- Our ranking for targeted keywords 'digital agency Gold Coast' went from thirteenth to second place, and 'marketing agency Gold Coast' went from fifty-first to sixth place.

- Our overall website traffic increased by up to 300%.

- Our brand had never been stronger, with direct traffic and searches for the word MeMedia indicating an all-time high.

What was our investment? We invested AUD $60,000 and got back $120,000 in sales in just one year. This was the only marketing we did at the time. That's a 100% return on marketing investment (ROMI).

Another client joined us in 2017. First we needed to rebuild their website into an ecommerce site, enabling people to purchase tickets online, and then to commence content marketing. We launched their new website in October 2017 and then got straight into implementing our PROACTIVE content marketing methodology. In April 2018, we took stock of where we were. The various areas had each had a similar size marketing investment, and their return on marketing was as follows:

- Organic: 6,736.34% ROMI

- Adwords: 501.13% ROMI

- Social: 600.55% ROMI

- All combined: 2,166.38% ROMI

Two years later, we've seen further increases and believe we still have room to grow.

Content marketing assets vs advertising liabilities

Another way of looking at marketing is to put your marketing and advertising activities into two different categories of asset or liability. Marketing assets and liabilities don't have quite the same definition as they do in finance or accounting terms, but this analogy can offer a different perspective on how we in the marketing world see our activities.

I define marketing assets as an activity, product or piece of content that, once produced, appreciates in value long after you've made the initial investment. The growth may be in the number of people who use that asset to discover you/your business, or who subscribe, or even the number of people who purchase. Examples include:

- Our website
  - Blogs
  - Videos
  - Infographics
  - White papers
  - Ebooks
- Online courses
  - Podcasts/YouTube shows
  - Social media profiles/pages
  - Guest appearances on podcasts or YouTube shows
  - Paid advertorials or news/PR in online publications
  - Physical items
  - Educational brochures
- Books
- Branded industry awards or Momentos (not to be confused with merchandise)

- Netflix/Amazon Prime/Stan documentaries or movies

I define a marketing liability as something that has a finite life or that requires more time or money spent on it to keep it alive, for example:

- TV advertising

- Radio advertising

- Google advertising

- Social media advertising

- Ads that don't grow in visible public engagement (ie users cannot see the huge number of likes or comments associated with the ad or piece of content)

- Physical magazine advertising or editorial

- Bus/billboard advertising

- Sporting team sponsorship.

If it wasn't for the internet, we would have little to compare here. When reviewing the lists above, we also have far more opportunity to create assets than we do liabilities. Not all of these assets will perform as well if they are not supported by injecting some advertising dollars into them to amplify their reach and engagement, but by doing so we are building something we and others can leverage at any time.

A simple way to distinguish a marketing asset from a liability is to track its usage over time and see how long you spent on that specific item.

Below is one of my favourite graphs, from a client we have been working with since 2016. It shows the number of page views for a single blog, which is hosted on our client's website and is one of around seventy pieces of content driving around 100 visitors daily.

In April 2016, we see an initial spike, which is the content release on social media and the paid amplification which we carried on until June 2016. From July 2016 onwards, there was no additional advertising spend and all traffic received by this blog was organic – unpaid traffic.

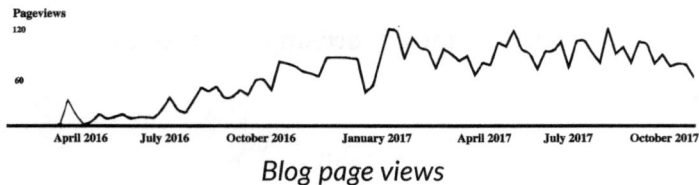

Blog page views

This one piece of content exists in an ecosystem we have created, a content-rich website full of articles, videos and infographics. Some of them assist in repeatedly directing traffic to this blog but all are classed as marketing assets. They have all had a similar amount of effort and advertising dollars applied and all have continued to grow the number of visits received. That's what I call a marketing asset – content which visibly increases in its usage or shows value to users, years after its creation.

Content marketing is holistic

The concept that content marketing is holistic (which I have always thought should be spelled 'wholistic' to better represent its meaning) is best described when referring to both our methodology and this Venn diagram, as we combine services which have traditionally been segregated and even managed by disparate people and/or agencies.

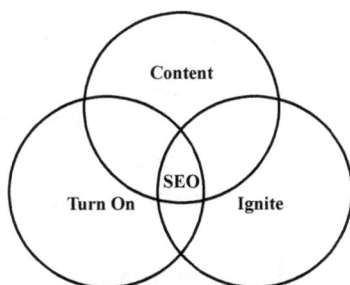

Skill sets and marketing roles

This diagram describes the skill sets and traditional marketing roles where content is written, designed or produced. It is then turned on/distributed via social media marketing, public relations-style activities or direct email/mail. Igniting your content with paid advertising spend and know-how is used to amplify the reach and engagement of the content and ideally gather leads on platforms or drive traffic to a landing page or blog. SEO is required to ensure the barriers to getting on the page (regardless of the device) and achieving the campaign goal are minimised.

SEO in brief

Many people believe they only need SEO or social media marketing or Google advertising. Given that content marketing is holistic, it makes room for all these tactics and skill sets.

SEO is the practice of attracting unpaid/organic traffic to your website and improving your conversion rate and search engine rankings. It is quite technical in nature and on its own does a great job of ensuring your website has the best possible chance of attracting and converting your traffic into customers or subscribers.

First, let's talk about Google Analytics. We have Google Analytics to thank for being able to effectively analyse our data. It was launched in 2005 and since then every website owner has installed this free tool on their website so that they can see exactly what's going on. That means Google knows what every website on the internet is doing and can use that data to determine which one deserves to be in the top position on Google for any specific search term.

There are other tools out there to analyse user behaviour and websites, but Google talks a language we need to understand and there are only a few tools which know how to speak that language. I'll list some other valuable tools at the end of the book.

SEO activities include:

- On page
  - Keywords, meta title, H1, page structure
  - Internal linking
  - Click-through conversion optimisation
  - Landing/sales page conversion optimisation
  - Cart/checkout conversion optimisation
- Technical
  - Website structure/information architecture
  - Usability testing and improvements
  - Sitemaps
  - Structured data (providing explicit clues about the meaning of a page to Google)
  - Rich snippets and other valuable meta tags
  - Duplicate content

- Site/page speed

- Mobile optimisation

- Off page

  - Google reviews

  - Sometimes DNS

  - Geographic hosting location

  - Authority of referring websites

- Analytics

  - Keyword research

  - Competitor website research

  - Comparison and analysis of before and after website performance

  - Conversion rate, visitor time on page, new vs return

  - Page views, time on site

  - Bounce rate, user flow

  - Referral links/backlinks

This may not be an exhaustive list but you can see that SEO can not only help improve your rankings but also your landing page conversions.

There was a time when finding and reaching out to other website owners to request that they link to you also fell under the SEO banner. This was commonly called backlinking, link building or a backlink outreach service. They are called backlinks because a website links back to you. Backlinks are valuable. They can still provide your website with traffic and they also give Google an indication that your site is being linked to. If it is, it's possible its rank should be increased on Google so that more people can see this content.

Good backlinks include links from government or education websites (hosted on a .gov or .edu domain) and reputable news websites, with a maximum of two links per domain counted towards improving your domain authority.

In 2014, Matt Cutts, the head of Google's Webspam team, stated that guest blogging for the purpose of link building is equivalent to outright spamming.[35] Cutts highlighted the fact that many SEO experts use guest blogging as an underhand way to build links and to increase traffic, rather than to engage viewers with quality content. How will his opinion impact upon SEO and guest blogging in the future?

Cutts has said that there are an increasing number of guest blogs being written for the sole purpose of SEO – to influence a website's ranking. This practice violates Google's guidelines, which are set up to help Google find and index a website. This means that embedded within the guest blog are hyperlinks to external websites that not only allow viewers to go directly to that external website, but more importantly allow search engines to follow the link. Google views links to other websites as a vote of confidence in the destination website and the more links to a website, the greater the page ranking.

Guest posts have been used to build SEO links to external websites for no other purpose than increasing the websites' page ranking in Google. There is nothing wrong with a link to a guest blogger's website. The issue is that many guest blogs are becoming more about chasing links than sharing quality content with people.

However, guest blogs are still a great way to engage both customers and people with similar interests, and there are two simple ways to make sure that you use guest blogging safely.

One is SEO and link building. If you are a guest blogger, make sure you write quality content that helps, educates, inspires or interests the reader. If you are a webmaster and accept guest blogs, ensure you have full confidence in the guest blogger's integrity. The aim of guest blogging is to interact with the audience and build meaningful relationships, rather than to write boring content with the sole aim of SEO link building through a back door.

The other method is using nofollow links. If you are confident that the links in a guest blog are natural and there is no intent to increase page ranking, there is no reason to use the nofollow tag. The nofollow tag is a piece of code that tells Google to not follow that particular link to the external website. This is important when money changes hands, such as in advertisements or affiliate links. It is also a great way to discourage spam comments on your website or blog.

Guest blogging has a solid place on the internet, but make sure it is of high quality and engages your audience, and avoid spammy, low-quality SEO content that simply chases the link.

Google's ranking algorithm is a complex beast, with over 200 ranking factors which decide what position your website should rank in; it is alleged that nobody outside of Google knows what all of those ranking factors are. Like many marketers who've been around for some time, I have figured out several activities which make a difference and several visible ways to measure your performance.

Some of you will be saying, 'Who cares about Google?' There are plenty of other ways people can discover and engage with your business that have nothing to do with Google. I agree, which is why we're never just focusing on SEO, but the acts of SEO are extremely valuable to all our other marketing activities.

However, the fact that 86% of internet searches are performed on Google means there's a rather large audience here. The second largest search engine in the world is YouTube, so it's worth making use of.[36]

Strategic and proactive marketing

When challenging yourself to accomplish any task or goal, is there any other way to be than proactive? Steven Covey, in his acclaimed book, *The 7 Habits of Highly Effective People*, lists 'be proactive' as habit number one.

Marketing can require a similar approach. Reactive marketing is generally performed too late, chasing the shiny marketing channel which has been touted to serve up customers on a platter, and execution is often under-resourced.

Reactive marketing is often implemented without a strategy, without research and without purpose, often via traditional advertising methods that only work through unappealing or unfavourable tactics and requesting that you 'buy now'.

PROACTIVE content marketing is a culmination of over twenty years of my own marketing execution in its various forms. It hasn't existed in its entirety for that time but has become a model which is far more strategic in nature than it is tactical.

The reason I felt this method was needed was two-fold. First, I wanted to be able to provide predictable and reliable results for my clients. Second, I felt that the strategic marketing methods I'd read or seen were not well thought out enough to allow for quick execution by the marketing team.

I'm often asked, 'Which is more important, strategy or execution?' and my answer is based on a story of my own journey in marketing. Since the beginning of my career, I'd been highly tactical, executing the marketing activities I was asked to do by my clients such as designing and programming ecommerce websites, or producing graphics, blogs and videos. In the early days of working in the trenches, executing, I knew all the technical tricks on how and why a website needs to be in the middle of marketing activity, but I wasn't aware of the overarching strategy. How did this blog or advertisement, on this website, contribute to the monthly, quarterly or annual strategic goals?

Most of the books I read on strategy gave great business advice but didn't offer a strategic marketing framework I could work with. Searching for 'marketing strategy templates' also produced poor or inconsistent results, without much explanation as to why this method is best.

The strategic PROACTIVE marketing method is a nine-step formula used for both marketing strategy development and execution. If we can create a marketing strategy document using the following headings as our structure, we can use the same formula each month or quarter to plan our campaigns.

PROACTIVE PLANNER	CAMPAIGN	PERIOD
P Purpose	**R** Research	**O** Opportunity
A Audience	**C** Content	**T** Turn On
I Ignite	**V** Verification & Validation	**E** Evolve

The one-page PROACTIVE Planner

For you to create the marketing strategy, in the following chapters I explain the function of each step. In some cases, I have developed a secondary framework to further assist our understanding of what's required.

SIX

Purpose

Our purpose encapsulates our values to inspire ourselves and our team, but it is also the perspective and life blood which inspire our tone of voice and where we're speaking from. If you run an accounting firm that helps families live a worry-free life because someone who loves numbers has devised a way of better money management, the purpose statement might be: 'Family-friendly worry-free money management.'

This gives the feeling of being nurtured and cared for by a professional who's taking away pain – money management. We know it's family oriented, friendly and if it's worry-free then the theme of the content will more likely be educational and inspirational without creating confusion. It will have to be precise, simple to understand and offer examples, which may be funny or at the very least entertaining.

Copywriting requires emotion to be expressed via emotive words and can also be built by setting up a story or landscape for people to relate to. Social media has encouraged us to express what we want to say in 140 characters or fewer, but even Twitter admitted that didn't work when they doubled it to 280 characters. That's still not enough.

Writing good copy that tells a story, is educational, inspirational and entertaining is difficult, but with the right purpose and tone of voice, and with no expectation or word limit, it can feel easier and far more authentic.

Most C-level managers won't have time or creative space to create 'works of art'. Knowing your purpose and values and having these available to share via a strategy document or video enables managers to bring professional copywriters or new recruits under their wing and guide them to produce beautiful content in an efficient and consistent manner.

The challenge of producing content is not limited to writing copy but also producing infographics and video. Your tone of voice cannot and should not falter when creating content on purpose. Consistency is key. Before we create any content, I've developed a structured way to 'discover' our brand purpose.

We discussed earlier in the book the process for getting your team and customers in the room following a SWOT analysis. Creating consistent, quality results requires a simple structure. The six Ps will help to define an organisation's purpose:

- Purpose and values

- Problem

- People

- Planet

- Product

- Profit

Purpose and values

Your personal purpose, values and passion often go hand in hand. They are the essential ingredients we all need to create a life worth living, which obviously connects with our working life.

I've included the following questionnaire on the PRO-ACTIVE marketing website under downloads. Visit www.proactivemarketing.co/downloads.

Questions to ask your team and customers:

- When you were growing up, who was the person you admired the most? Who is/was your hero?

- Could you use the values list to identify at least ten to twenty of their values?

- What are your top twenty personal values?

- Which five must exist within your place of work? They don't have to be the same.

- What activities within your job role fulfil these values?

- What job-related tasks do you feel you must perform weekly to ensure you're living out your values?

- When you're not at work, what adventures do you crave?

- Who do you like to enjoy these adventures with most?

- Who are your favourite authors, actors, musicians or sports celebrities?

Problem

Solving problems is what every product or service does, but not all are problems worth solving, nor are they backed by market research.

The questions we ask the team are:

1. What problem does the business solve?

2. What problem do you solve within the business?

3. What does your solution mean to others within the business? How does it help them do their job?

4. What supporting roles/functions do you think are needed to best solve this problem (existing or additional)?

The questions we ask our customers are similar but with some variations:

1. What are your top three problems in your business, which may or may not be related to this business relationship?

2. What problem do you have that you need the serving business to help solve?

3. What do you value most when dealing with this business?

4. What positive feeling do you wish to be left with long after the purchase is complete?

People

Who do we solve our problems for? How many other people solve this problem and how to solve this problem will dictate your future success.

Team questions:

- Who (individual person) do you feel needs you most at work? What position do they hold?
- Describe a time when you displayed your best personal qualities when working under time pressures with a co-worker.
- What emotional qualities do you possess that make you the best person for dealing with daily challenges at work?
- Who does the company solve problem(s) for? How would you describe them? What is their title?
- How long does the positive feeling of our product last and why?

Customer questions:

- Are you the decision maker making the purchase?

- Are you the first point of call when dealing with the business you're purchasing from? If not, name the person(s) who may continue the relationship.

- When dealing with a similar business, what is it that turns you off?

- What beliefs do you have when dealing with businesses like this?

- What is the single defining value that would convince you this is the right place for you to purchase from?

- Do you think this is a one-time purchase or do you expect to purchase other products/services?

- What time(s) of year do you normally make this type of purchase?

Planet

So long as it is the secondary benefit of doing business with you, it helps that your purpose aligns with a local, global or industry-related cause. This helps reinforce that you have a purpose beyond profit, even though your purpose is to serve the customer first.

Team and customer questions:

- What local, industry or planetary problem might benefit from the way you produce your product or service?

- How does the planet benefit from you producing your product the way you produce it?

- What group of people or organisations (on the planet) benefit from you producing your best product?

- What group of people would rally behind you and support you to produce your product?

- How could you categorise or describe these people?

- How do your team and customers expect you to produce your product? This could mean in terms of ethical manufacturing, whether it's manufactured or produced locally or if it is done offshore.

- What charity or cause do you resonate with the most, given your own life experiences?

- What planetary cause(s) are too far removed from your own personal purpose?

Product

Defining the generic term for the product you produce can help reduce confusion when educating your customers. Often, the more scientific the description for your product is, the more you confuse the customer. For example, 'wildlife conservation' is understood less than 'caring for wildlife'.

Team questions:

1. What is your contribution to producing the organisation's product?

2. What does the organisation's product mean to your customers?

3. Is the transaction between you and your customers short lived or long term?

4. What is the most important quality or value of the product you produce?

5. How are you best appreciated within the business? By who, and with what?

Customer questions:

1. How do you feel when you purchase the product?

2. What weight is lifted off your shoulders when you make the purchase?

3. How does the purchase of this product affect others who might be impacted by this purchase?

4. How does the purchase of this product make you 'look' good in the eyes of others?

Profit

Regardless of what type of business or organisation you operate, making a profit is important, as is knowing your profit margin on products and overall organisational profit. I have known businesses to spend anywhere from 5% to 12% of turnover on their marketing and advertising, with the average being closer to 8%. A donation to a charity or cause can fluctuate from month to month but most businesses follow the 1% rule for donations.

In January 2021, another of MeMedia's retailer clients developed a non-traditional sale campaign, which we called the %20$21 Giveback, where customers were offered 20% off select items and $21 of every sale was donated to a worthy cause, with an impressive total of $9,933 going to this cause.

Aside from the donation, the connection created with the community was astounding. Customers and team members all had stories which they shared with each other during the retail shopping experience.

After the cheque was handed over and photos taken, multiple government, community and news organisations shared the news. The donation recipients published an article which achieved more organic shares than any other social media post our client had shared in the past six months. The story hit the front page on the local weekend newspaper and the local MP announced the giveback to the state government.

While the press was well received, the customer engagement was the highlight. It connected our client's team members with their customers on a cause beyond the product they came to purchase. This connection was emotional more than transactional and as such will be everlasting.

The cause is not the purpose for which the customer initially engages your business but it becomes part of the lasting emotional connection to the purchase.

As mentioned above, using both the team and customers' answers from the six Ps will help to define your organisation's purpose and develop your marketing strategy.

Like all good wines and whiskeys, the final outcome comes from distilling the data down so that you can create your marketing strategy and campaign plans.

I have included the PROACTIVE marketing strategy template on the PROACTIVE marketing website under downloads so that you may take your raw data and fill in the blanks within this strategy document. Visit www.proactivemarketing.co/downloads.

Purpose: Marketing Strategy

- **Purpose:** describe your brand's purpose in a tagline and purpose statement, including the people you serve and the product if appropriate.
- **Values:** list up to six values and describe your consistent actions that ensure you live up to these values.
- **Problem:** what are the existing problems that your product/service will solve? Are they a people and/or a planetary problem?
- **Product:** what is the product you sell that solves the problem?
- **Profit:** voice the amount you plan to give to a charity or a cause based on criteria such as $1 for every product sold or 1% of revenue.

Purpose: Marketing Campaign Plan

- **Purpose:** describe the purpose of the campaign and how this ties back to your values or overarching brand purpose.

SEVEN

Research

Being inspired to create content because you have this gut feeling that you can do it better than anyone else is amazing. If I have an epiphany, I can't wait to scribble down my idea or brainstorm with the team on what we can create. I love getting carried away with cool ideas to produce content, so I constantly have to remind myself before sharing that my mind is operating in a vacuum.

Your idea might be the inspiration and the motivation to produce a certain style of content, but research best informs you as to what topics are worthy of this creative time. Creating the content first and then adapting it to the research is reactionary and not proactive, therefore not strategic.

The method I use when performing research is called PROBE, which stands for:

- **P**hrase
- **R**ight now
- **O**pinion
- **B**rand
- **E**xpression

Phrase

We need to know what people are currently searching for. Rather than focus on a single keyword, we need to understand the key phrases/multi-word search terms which are used to discover your business, product or service.

Asking your customers what they would type into Google to search for you is great research, but this doesn't always allow you to receive the quantity of answers needed to decide which search terms are more relevant to your product than others.

In 2010, Google removed the ability for marketers to see 100% of the search keywords users were typing into Google to get to your website. Google announced that this was for privacy reasons and stated that some information would be shared but that which is not shared will appear as 'not provided'.[37]

Eventually, 97% of the search keywords were 'not provided'. Marketers felt they had no alternative, but some cool tools came onto the scene and if you weren't disgruntled by Google making this change, Google Adwords has remained the most reliable source for understanding which keywords/phrases are most searched.

Adwords has to provide its advertisers with the keyword search terms which triggered the advertising, and while we all have to pay for this keyword data – instead of getting it for free all those years ago – we are able to use this system to our advantage.

Google Adwords gives us the ability to test keywords and content to match those search terms almost instantly (weeks instead of months), which can save many months in finding the answers to these questions:

- Does our audience even use Google to search for our product/service?

- What are the multi-word/long-tail search terms they're typing into Google?

- Are they more interested in finding us through Google Search, the Display Network, YouTube or Google Maps?

Once your adwords have been running for a few weeks, you can start to analyse the keywords and phrases that are popular, determine if they're driving business as well as traffic and use these insights to help create topical content.

Google Adwords is great at validating keywords and whether they are worth investing in for SEO. For instance, if we discovered through our adwords advertising that getting clicks to our site for a certain search term only resulted in people clicking our ad and bouncing, and we have pretty solid proof that this phrase is not resulting in any conversions (because it may be associated with an alternate industry or search term that is completely unrelated to our business), we may be better off not spending time and money creating content around this. Our end goal is to increase our Google ranking and get organic traffic.

If you're not a fan of Google or don't have the budget, there are other paid tools that do a great job of showing what keywords/phrases people are typing into Google that lead them to click on your site, such as Keyword Hero and SEMrush.

In 2020, Google announced they would start restricting insights into what keywords triggered your advertisements, which is inconvenient for marketers and advertisers. Using multiple tools to perform your keyword discovery is advised.

A combination of adwords campaigns and the Google Adwords Keyword Tool plus MOZ and SEMrush and a bit of spreadsheeting gets the best results for us. Using this method, we're able to find out the monthly search volume and the competition for the search term (ie how hard it is going to be for us to get a good ranking and also how much we might need to pay per click).

If we already have pages on our site(s) which we can direct these new search terms to, we'll want to take note of this in our audit and look to implement the keywords in our advertising and ensure we create the content on those pages to direct traffic to.

Right now

Where is our product/service right now in the innovation adoption lifecycle?

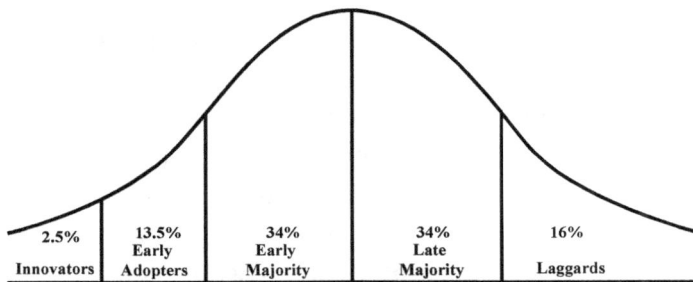

The innovation adoption lifecycle

Gathering insights from Google advertising campaign(s) and whether your audience even uses Google to search for your product/service can help determine what kind of audience you're marketing to.

If your product is cutting edge and innovative, you're going to be speaking to people who have never heard of your product or service before. Early adopters are slightly different and can be more easily convinced if they see your product/service is cool, edgy and has a high likelihood of doing the job.

The early majority like to see more proof than the previous two. The late majority and laggards are those who will only do it because their current one is broken and they have no choice but to move with the times.

Another way to consider what kind of market you're going to be delivering your message to is to find out whether you have an active audience or a dormant audience. Active audiences are actively searching, which means they already know your product or service exists. They just need to find the companies who sell the product or service and compare which one is right for them. Dormant audiences are those who are likely to have an interest in what you have to sell but don't know your product or service exists. The dormant market is where the future opportunity lies because they are seen as innovators or early adopters in their industry.

Balancing our strategy to meet both the active and dormant market allows us to bring balance to our strategy by not ignoring what business we could potentially get now and in the future. Couple this with the power of Google Trends and you can see not only the past but the future. Google Trends helps us determine if search terms which relate to our business are rising or falling.

Not all trends are crystal balls for the future. I'm sure Blackberry thought they were onto a winner around October 2008 when the trend for the term 'Blackberry' first peaked and then in 2012 it started its rapid descent.

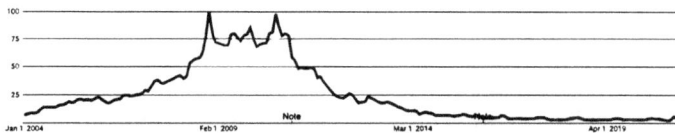

Blackberry search trends

You may also be speaking to a certain industry, which can change the stage of adoption they're at. If you're operating in an over-saturated market and it feels as if there is no one left to market to, there will always be an industry which lags behind the rest and it's entirely possible that they are now in the early adoption phase.

Another way of looking at this part of the process is to develop an understanding of how your products, services and/or consultancy stack up against your competitors'. This can be simply done in a spreadsheet.

Start this process by taking a bird's eye view of who in the world stands out as being in the top six companies. While they may be on a different scale to you, they should offer some insights into how and why they're operating the way they are.

List the products or services for each of the competitors across the rows from column B onwards. There is no limit to the categories you can list but keeping your options/columns lean will help you grasp this process much quicker than if you had ten or more.

Column A should be for your scale of measurement in terms of the visible marketing competitiveness each company has (scoring from 0–4).

With each line on your graph representing your top six companies, commence plotting their line by evaluating their score for each product/service category they offer. When you have completed each of your competitors, you can then establish what your strategic opportunity might be for your own products/services and whether you should compete on them or not.

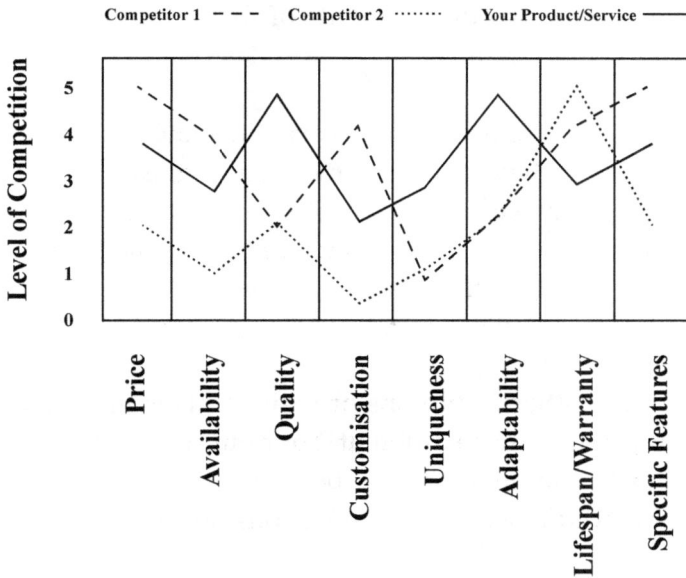

Scoring your competitors

Opinion

Who already has an opinion or viewpoint on this and how are they crafting this? By researching your competitive landscape, you will be able to see whether others are using the same terminology, features, materials and options as you and they will surely have an opinion on why the customer needs to purchase their product.

Once you've gathered your competitive research, you'll need to decide what approach you're willing to take. Are you going to add new features, increase the perceived value/benefits of their features or be competitive on price?

You could make an effort to explain something better than others have before. Some of the biggest mistakes marketers make include using too much industry jargon and too many acronyms, and explaining the features but not the benefits. Maybe they're not as charismatic as you, or maybe they're not being authentic.

Finding others' opinions or viewpoints is important but you have to be different. Your purpose and values can help differentiate you because your opinion can be skewed to your own life and business experience.

Brand

Is the keyword used to describe your product or service 'owned' by a brand you should attempt to hijack or disrupt? The competition is high and potentially there are a few brands that are almost at the point of owning the space you're playing in. The market may even be using their brand name or trademarked tagline as a verb. For example, 'Google it' or 'just do it'.

If the competing brand names are now verbs, my advice is not to try to compete but start collaborating or differentiate yourself completely. Giving up is not an option.

Has Microsoft given up on Bing? Have Adidas and Reebok given up on making shoes?

Sometimes it is possible to hijack a brand name within your content, especially when the name can be used in a sentence without it looking as if you're referring to the brand. One of my favourite electric skateboard brands is Evolve Skateboards, made here on the Gold Coast. They're constantly innovating, and new tech comes out every year that always seems better than the last. If I was their competitor, I'd be writing content which inserts the word 'evolve' into my copy. It's an English verb, after all, and no trademark lawyer would be able to refute that.

This keyword inclusion is not something that should be heavily focused on, but it can be employed to simply get noticed as an alternative brand option. It can also be used to ensure you squeeze out the smaller competition, who may try to leverage your brand name or tag line.

Companies have tried to hijack our brand name (MeMedia) and they were able to do so because one of our trademarks wasn't registered in a class that they managed to squeeze through. With some simple tweaks to words preceding our brand name and after our brand name, we managed to remove them from the top positions on Google.

Being the brand at the top of Google organic search results for your competitor's brand name is a win.

Expression

The other way to be competitive is to express yourself in a different medium to your competitors. What type of medium will you choose to express your expertise? Copy, graphics, photographs, video, animation – maybe even a book?

Often this is the most exciting way to improve brand engagement. My favourite tool to discover the different media opportunities is MOZ (or SEOMOZ). Based on certain keywords/phrases, MOZ has tools that tell you what content has been created using these terms, and video and graphics are nearly always underdone.

If you exist in a highly competitive landscape, I hope that using these five steps of research to PROBE your market helped you to see the multitude of options available to you to create content.

RESEARCH: Marketing Strategy

- **Phrase:** what are people searching for?
- **Right now:** what does Google Trends say?
- **Opinion:** who else is competing for these terms?
- **Brand:** can we/should we hijack a brand name?

- **Expression:** what media will we choose to express ourselves in?

RESEARCH: Marketing Campaign Plan

- What is this campaign's name or code name?
- What keywords/phrases must be included to support our SEO targets?
- Where is our audience in the adoption of this idea (innovation, early adoption, early majority, late majority, laggards)?
- Do we have to educate them or can we proceed assuming they understand?
- Does our opinion hold enough weight to sell the campaign?
- Do we have to back up this campaign with research or quotes from third parties?
- Are any other competing brands using this campaign name?
- Is the hashtag being used by anybody else?
- What mediums will be used to express the campaign (blogs, photographs, video)?

EIGHT

Opportunity

Seeing the opportunities which exist for you is not hard work, it's just time consuming. Knowing what you're looking for is half the battle. I use this method, known as IWIN, to establish what opportunities exist.

Insights

Start by detailing the insights our PROBE research gave us, such as the phrase we're going to target due to its high search volume, low competition and/or our potential to see a quick win. I use this term 'quick win' cautiously because getting immediate results from any type of marketing isn't possible. Everything requires time to strategise, create and embed itself into our potential customers' psyche before they act.

Digital marketing activities generally take three months to come to fruition. Saying that, if your website is ranking on page two within Google for specific keywords/phrases then it's logical for us to begin working on improving this rank as a priority keyword, as we can expect to see results earlier than if we were to focus on keywords which are off Google's radar.

Website/platform

We cannot leverage from an unstable platform. Our research may have led us to discover that we are not able to immediately embark on creating ongoing content because it's missing the essential page structure or technology needed to do that.

While rebuilding our platform is common, it's not always required, and when we are developing our strategy it's important to weigh up the short- and long-term benefits of delaying our marketing execution for this development. If you're considering rebuilding your platform (and your business can accept the delay), do it because it will become the catalyst for a well-oiled marketing machine.

Integrations

If MOZ has revealed that the media being used for content which targets the keyword is video, and your website is so out of date that we cannot easily embed a YouTube video, clearly you should consider fixing this.

Other integrations that may be required are landing page, scorecard software and automation software to capture and nurture leads which might be generated via website visitation.

Have you identified that creating an online course is essential or that you require a members' area? Are you planning on running monthly webinars or events which will require event registration software? These integrations are further opportunities for you to be able to execute your strategy.

Network

What physical and digital networks will you leverage during the marketing execution? Will you require a YouTube channel, LinkedIn page or TikTok? Google My Business posts and reviews are a must.

How will you engage your human network to help you reach outside your existing circles or further bolster your brand reputation? What industry bodies might you need to become a member of? Do you need to seek a position on the board of a charity or chamber of commerce?

It's easy to get caught up in the 'how'. Remember these are just a few points you've discovered might be important to consider because you noticed your competitors were or were not seeing this same opportunity.

OPPORTUNITY: Marketing Strategy

- Insights from our research
- Website/platform requirements
- Integrations we will need
- What networks we can leverage

OPPORTUNITY: Marketing Campaign Plan

- Based on our research, does our marketing foundation (ie website) support our campaign or do we need to adjust/make improvements?
- Do we require a specific landing page to be set up?
- Is there an opportunity for automation to be integrated?

NINE

Audience

The philosopher Epictetus supposedly said that 'we have two ears and one mouth so that we can listen twice as much as we speak'. When it comes to knowing your audience, data is everything. If you don't have it, you need to get it.

For every product or service you sell, there is the potential for a different audience. Every audience has different problems or reasons why they want your product/service and, if you don't know those problems, you cannot deliver a solution.

There is a lot of confusion around targeting and demographics. Millennials were born between the early 1980s and the year 2000. According to Roy Morgan Research, millennials make up around 4.9 million Australians,

Generation X makes up 4.8 million and baby boomers 4.1 million.[38] Generation Alpha are those born between 2010 and 2024 and are already among the influencers who guide the parents' buying decisions.

In a study, Deloitte describes millennials as the 'values generation'. [39] While the study focuses on employment of millennials, it also tells us a lot about how this generation functions in everyday life. Millennials want business to shift its purpose. While they continue to express a positive view of business's role in society and have softened their negative perceptions of business motivation and ethics compared to prior services, millennials still want businesses to focus more on people, employees, customers, society, products and purpose and less on profits.

What does this tell us about how millennials choose brands? We need to have a purpose beyond profit, and we need to clearly articulate why our business exists. How are you going to express all this in your marketing? Millennials are the digital generation, which means they're using their smartphones to communicate via Facebook, Instagram, Snapchat, TikTok, LinkedIn, Clubhouse and YouTube.

With 2.7 billion monthly active users, more than a third of the world's population uses Facebook; 77% of them are millennials, eighteen to thirty-four-year-olds, compared to 68% of thirty-five to fifty-four-year-olds and 52% of the 55+ demographic.[40, 41]

The second most popular social media channel among millennials is Instagram. According to the 2020 Consumer Culture Report, 70% use it daily, with 39% of thirty-five to fifty-four-year-olds also using Instagram daily, but just 9% of 55+ use it this often.[42]

If we jump over to the business focus social media platform LinkedIn, we can see that there are 87 million millennials using this platform, but all of these statistics on how you're going reach your target audience mean nothing unless you've defined your brand's purpose and can communicate that via storytelling or through useful content that will bring a change to the world. This brings us back to why content marketing is the best type to focus on, and YouTube is a great place to do this.

In 2014, Google partnered with TNS and Ogilvy to answer questions about what brand advertisers can do to connect with millennials. The study revealed that consumers choose the brands that engage them in their passions and interest 42% more often than they do those that simply urge them to buy the product being advertised.[43] As a result, their path to purchase is actually their path to purpose.

The same study revealed that consumers are 70% more likely to purchase something with a brand that engages people on their purpose and their passions. YouTube found that users aged between eighteen and thirty-four are four times more interested in watching a video ad on YouTube than viewing on any other platform.

Statistics from the 5WPR 2020 Consumer Culture Report revealed that YouTube is the third most used social platform among millennials, with 66% of the eighteen- to thirty-five-year-olds surveyed for the report using it daily.[44]

It's clear from that last bit of research that content marketing via video and uploading to YouTube could be a perfect strategy for everybody, but it's not just video that is working out there in the marketplace.

Look at infographics and photo-heavy blogs. Instead of me telling you that you have to go and produce this amazing content right now, I want you to come back to some of the grassroots preparation everybody needs to do before entering into a content marketing campaign:

- Define and document your core values, your purpose and your cause.

- Understand why your existing customers do business with you and how this relates to your values.

- Discover what secrets you or your company hold that could make your industry a better place to work if they were shared openly for the uninitiated to learn from.

- What valuable lessons can your clients teach the world and how did you work with them to make their business/life more successful/meaningful?

While going through this process, you'll begin to structure your business in a way that focuses less on your profits and more about the change you bring to the world.

A natural way to find an audience if you're B2B (business to business) is to start investigating companies, their size, geographic location, their service area and what problems you can identify that you may be able to solve. We need to establish contact with these brands, which means talking to people.

Whether you're B2B or B2C (business to consumer) we are really performing human to human (H2H) marketing. We can't develop a relationship with a logo, nor can a physical product answer our questions. We must simply talk to people, ask important questions and listen twice as much as we talk.

How do we best get to know our audience?

- Talk to them. Preferably in person.

- Talk to people/businesses/publications who already have your audience as a customer.

- Gather data from:

  – Competition entries

  – Research studies

  – Social media and search advertising analytics

Ask these questions to identify demographics:

- What are we trying to find out?

- How old are they?

- Where do they live?

- How much money do they make?

- Do they have kids?

- Is it a dual-income household?

Demographics are less important than psychographics. Psychographics is the study and classification of people according to their likes, attitudes, interests, aspirations and other psychological criteria such as their values.

Combining these psychographics with the questions we asked in the earlier customer workshop will be far more beneficial than demographics. This is important because, if you start to place an advertisement on social media, you need to know the behaviours, attitudes, interests and lifestyle of your audience to target them.

Aside from being able to set up your social media audiences quicker, you're better able to understand what makes your customer tick, enabling you to become more empathetic in both the content you create and the sales process.

Online and telephone surveys are already a thing of the past and unless you're offering a worthwhile incentive for people to spend their precious spare time talking to you, it's hard to get the information you need. This method can be impersonal and normally run by a call centre or online system, which can also create annoyance barriers between you and your customer.

Talking to people in person is the best way every time. Here are the questions I like to ask:

- What are some of your favourite things to do when it's only you that you have to worry about (and not kids, spouse, work, bills, housework, etc)?

- What are three to five of your favourite movies, actors, authors and musicians?

- Who did you admire most when you were growing up?

- What did you admire about them?

- What are two things you love that you believe define your happiness?

- What are two things that annoy you most about the world/work right now?

- Do you have any ideas on how you can directly impact/make a difference here?

- What is your favourite brand and why?

- Do you have a favourite social media at the moment?

- What do you like to do on this social media? Post? Comment? Message? Watch?

- Do you play sport or have any outside activities you like to do?

- Why does this bring you joy? Friends? Fitness? Strategic thinking? Creativity?

- What's your ideal holiday?

- What's your ideal way to spend a Sunday?

- Do you feel your work encourages you to be your best self? Why?

- Do you ever do personal shopping/jobs during business hours?

- If so, is that via your work computer or a personal device?

- Does anything about getting things done online annoy you?

- Are you an early riser or late to bed?

- What is your first activity on a weekday morning vs the weekend?

Sometimes it's difficult to talk with other businesses who have your ideal audience as their customer, but this is an opportunity to potentially collaborate. This business may have goods or services that can be leveraged as competition gifts in seasonal promotions, which opens the doors for both companies to benefit by obtaining customer contact data.

Publications should have a media kit which describes their own research findings or research from reputable sources – their audience demographics and psychographics. They may even know about seasonal highs and lows that you have not previously been aware of.

Whether you advertise or not is a different matter. The data is what is important at this stage because knowing that the publication appeals to your customer allows you to know what kind of content they are interested in. Asking about their best-selling issue or best-performing advertorial can help you develop a theme for your own content.

Your audience research should help you understand that you have different audiences that are interested in different products. You'll need to develop personas for each audience type. The most common way to define each persona is to give them a name and insert a photo of them into your persona profile alongside all the demographic and psychographic answers to the questions you've asked.

Limiting your number of personas to a maximum of four is generally best in the short term. In the B2B world, you might have the following personas to market to:

- Project Manager Pete

- HR Helen

- Financial Fred

- Sales Manager Steve

In the B2C world it could be:

- Johnny Junior

- Teenage Tracy

- Millennial Mark

- Baby Boomer Betty

Note that just because I named these personas based on the demographic, that doesn't mean you should neglect their psychographics.

I've included a one-page persona template for you to download from www.proactivemarketing.co /downloads.

AUDIENCE: Marketing Strategy

- Develop a one-page profile for each persona you'll be targeting.

AUDIENCE: Marketing Campaign Plan

- List which persona(s) you'll target for this campaign.

TEN

Content

This is the part where we get to have the most fun: content creation. Now is the time to decide whether your content is going to educate, entertain or inspire your audience, or even if it's going to be a triple threat – when you combine all three. But all that content creation can mean nothing if the motivations behind its creation are wrong.

How many times have you shared content which is completely sales focused? How often do you stop reading or watching a piece of content if there's a request to sign up? Do you skip ads? Are you creating content that is truly going to help your target audience? Or are you creating it for selfish reasons? What is the purpose of your content? Is it to get more sales? To create more leads?

If the main reason you're creating content is to get more traffic to your website, get people to buy more, or get more people to sign up, then you're off track. Your visitors are supposed to be engaging with your content but instead of finding gold, they're finding fool's gold.

Creating content which is a triple threat isn't easy. It requires serious creativity, guts and skill, especially when you're looking to produce video content with emotional engagement. This is where we need to tap into our values and purpose as these can help us define the genre of our content.

Earlier we looked at the marketing assets which are ideal to host on your website and/or make up your marketing collateral:

- Blogs

- Videos

- Photos

- Infographics

- White papers

- Ebooks

Creating an emotional connection can be done with every type of content, but film is by far the most engaging. An emotional connection occurs when people connect their values, desires or aspirations to a brand.

Sometimes these connections live in the unconscious mind and are hard to describe, because they are stored in what is known as the limbic brain. 'The limbic brain is responsible for all of our feelings, such as trust and loyalty...but it has no capacity for language,' says Simon Sinek. 'This is where "gut decisions" come from. They just feel right.'[45]

Which emotion are you going to attempt to tap into? Joy, sadness, fear, anger, disgust, surprise, trust, envy, love? The emotion you wish to convey should depend on your values – often a specific value which inspires your purpose – and can be best portrayed by storytelling. If you have charitable values, share how you are not only helping your customer but also your charity, or how your customers can help them by doing business with you. For example, your goal may be to help X number of people/animals every time somebody does business with you.

How many pieces of content can you create which tell this story before it gets boring? You could do it two or three times to begin with, showing how you're helping, and then insert your cut-down purpose statement at the end of your content.

Not all content has to be emotional. To educate, inspire or entertain is where you will start, so you can breathe a sigh of relief – you're not going to have to create award-winning content straight out of the gates.

The simplest of these is education. You're a professional, after all, and you have intellectual property (IP) sitting in that brain of yours or among your team or systems that already benefits your existing customers. If you share this information, it may inspire potential customers to do business with you and it may also show your competitors how you operate.

Reviewing products and services that are valuable to your existing clients is a great way to keep your existing clients engaged. Maybe they'll share it with their friends, which could mean more new clients for you. Your motivation behind creating that review is to be truly helpful. Mentioning somebody else's product is also a great way to potentially create a new partnership. Send them a link or tag them in social media – maybe they'll share it with their audience as well. You could increase your reach dramatically.

You may get asked the same questions a lot by your existing clients. It's about time you turned those questions into an awesome piece of content – a blog, infographic or video. Questions get asked on the internet all the time. How? Why? Where? Who? Having a library of frequently asked questions (FAQ) on your website will be a goldmine for your customers. If your customers are asking questions, many others might be too. Where do we go when we've got a question? Google.

This is the point where many people I speak to on this matter check out. 'No way am I sharing my secrets of how I run my business,' I hear them say. 'My competitors will use them against me.' While your competitors might try to use your IP against you, it's hard to do that when yours is publicly promoted and theirs is not. Your IP most likely stems from years of working in the industry or because you happened to stumble upon a business opportunity, did a truckload of research, developed a business/software application around it and went to market.

How many of your competitors could say they did it the exact same way as you? Which of your competitors have exactly the same ideas? They will have similar ideas if they learned them from the same person you did, but if you have the mental scars, the runs on the board and the case studies to prove you learned this way of business on your own, it's time to tell the world.

Your competitors may try to copy you, but if you produce great content consistently for years to come, you will have the advantage. By the time they've realised what you're doing, they will already be a minimum of three to twelve months behind.

Remember, consistency matters. It's the consistency of releasing content for years which truly builds a brand. Once you attract your audience and have them engaging with your content, they will come to expect it from you. They will rely on you for the education, inspiration or entertainment every month and if you don't deliver, they will begin to wonder why you stopped. Stopping can be more detrimental to your brand than not producing content at all. Your goal is to stay ahead of your competitors, inform your existing and potential customers and do so for as long as you're in business.

Blogging

Video is by far the best content medium to create, but blogs can go a long way, and I always recommend brands start here.

Regardless of what generation you're targeting, there are plenty of people who enjoy reading and do so because they like to understand every detail of what you're saying. They like to use it as reference material or ways to better inform their audience or boss. It's easy to copy and paste and to be plagiarised, but that is not your concern.

Once upon a time, SEO experts figured out that if you stuffed keywords into a piece of content, Google would rank you for those keywords. If you lived through this period of Black Hat SEO, you will recall all sorts of strange occurrences of keywords being forcefully stuffed into sentence after sentence and even more keywords appearing in bulk at the footer of an article.

While having a keyword or two in your blog is important, the main thing to remember is that you want people to read your content and enjoy it.

SEO is one area I questioned myself on back in 1998 when I was creating my first websites for clients. There was nowhere near as much information available on the topic as there is now and I was uncertain as to how I should be creating websites (as opposed to how I was actually creating them). I didn't bother with keyword stuffing. I just created content and websites with the minimum number of keywords and remained consistent on publishing that content. It wasn't until years later that I discovered I was doing it right all along. Worrying about SEO was a total waste of time.

Today, the same rules ring true. Write for the user, not the robot (Google). There are no hard and fast rules for how many words you write but keep in mind that your goal when writing is to keep people engaged for minutes, not seconds. Spending time with people is your concern and if we're going to aim to spend seven hours with people, we're going to want our blogs to either be long or frequent in their release. Blogs can be written as short pieces of content if you're offering a summary of previous events with links to those longer pieces you've written before. More often than not, you're going to be aiming for 1,000 words.

Your content should also use the science of skimming. Make sure to include one level one heading in your content and multiple level two and three headings. Take the opportunity to bold words so that, if a website visitor just read the headings and the bolded words, they would get the general gist of what is being said. Use diagrams, embedded video, screenshots, photographs and graphs where possible and link to other pages on your website from within the paragraph text.

Linking to external sources is great too but be careful not to direct your visitors to another website without giving them a reason to stay on yours. For example, you might link to a research study which bolsters your argument, but most studies are hard to read. If you make your article easier to read than the research study, you've already won.

Your values and purpose inspire your brand's tone of voice, which is how your content will remain consistent. I'm not saying you have to refer to your charity, cause or purpose beyond profit in every blog post, but your visitors should be able to feel the same human qualities across your content.

Infographics

Infographics are a great way to summarise a long-form blog into a piece of content that can be consumed and understood in thirty seconds. This is why consumers love them too – infographics break down a complex topic and make it simple. When you release an info-graphic, you should always have 'infographic' in the title, or at least a picture of the infographic in your thumbnail, as the click-through will be far greater if you do.

Infographics should not exist on their own. They inspire your visitors to want to read more. Insert your info-graphic at the top of a blog you've already written, and you can distribute the same URL you did last month but with a new way for your audience to understand the topic.

Infographics are also the best way to storyboard an animation. By spending time mapping out the steps in a process or an orderly way of doing things in a single graphic, they can then be easily tweaked and fixed before embarking on the creation of your animated video.

Ebooks or white papers

Ebook and white paper downloads have been around for as long as I've been working in marketing and have been used mostly in B2B sales. They are normally in PDF format and have a form asking for your details or even a payment before you're able to download the PDF.

This tactic is commonly used for lead generation, as anybody who's interested in downloading the content could be interested in doing business with you.

When you enter your details, you're either let straight into the content page or you're emailed a link to where you can download or read the content. Anybody who enters their details knows they're likely to get a salesperson calling them and pestering them to spend money. If you send people straight to the page versus sending them a link, your data is going to be littered with fake names, emails and phone numbers.

Does this matter? Not really. Those who are fine with being contacted will put their correct details in and expect a call. But if you're anything like me, incomplete or unreliable data makes my head spin. I prefer to inform people that they will be emailed or sent an SMS with the link rather than being let straight into the content. This way they have to at least enter a valid email address and/or phone number, and I have some idea that this person is real instead of a potential script being run by a nuisance marketer or hacker.

Animated videos

Animations have always been one of my favourite ways to articulate a complex procedure or creatively tell a story using avatars, graphs or drawn objects to support the audio narration. In content marketing, they are valuable for education.

Animations are particularly useful in the medical industry. We can explain a medical procedure such as an orthopaedic knee or hip replacement surgery and do it without any live footage. By showing the patient a visual representation of what they can expect – without the realism of blood and bones – the patient can psychologically distance themselves from the reality of what's about to happen but still be well informed and prepared.

The construction industry has been using animations for some time, and for decades airlines have been showing passengers infographic-style safety cards, which could be turned into an animation.

Whether you're crafting a 2D or 3D animation, the time to produce them is far greater than an infographic or motion picture film. A well-crafted one-minute animation could easily take up to eighty hours to produce and, given the need to release content consistently, the time devoted to this could affect your content release schedule. While I love animation, I would always plan to release blogs, an infographic or motion picture film while the animation is being crafted.

Animation can also be used in conjunction with motion picture film to overlay diagrams, graphs, words or objects that assist with educational content. With more special effects, we can take our educational piece and provide some entertainment and inspirational values. To do this well, you will require what is known as a green screen, in front of which the presenter is filmed, and then in the edit you can replace the green with any image or video you like.

Video

Apart from being able to build an emotional connection with the audience, it is simple with video to bring yourself closer to your potential customer and there are many ways to do it.

This is where storytelling becomes more story showing. If you take the time to produce a film that has visuals to support your story, you're going to be far happier with the outcome and you can expect your audience to be more engaged.

When creating a romantic, dramatic, funny or exciting film for your audience, it's easy to get carried away and want to turn your production into a masterpiece, suitable for television or the big screen, but this is where production can come unstuck. We must remember where our audience are and what they are going to appreciate. You'll need to capture their attention in the first three seconds, set up the storyline in the next twelve seconds and then deliver on your promise for the next minute or minute and fifteen seconds.

While video is great, we watch a lot of it on our smart devices while we are at lunch, travelling or in the bathroom. People like to multi-task and if the toilet is the only place they feel they can escape the daily grind and watch something which entertains them, they're probably going to take this opportunity. Given the device and the timing of when people consume the content, we have to ensure we're getting the most bang for our buck as the producers of the content. We need people to engage with the content and that can be as simple as watching the video to the end.

The online video space is bursting at the seams, offering so many spaces for video ads that brands and agencies still struggle to understand how the digital space differs from running television commercials.

Google's Unskippable Labs continually run experiments with brands and agencies to test what works best. Ben Jones, global creative director at Unskippable Labs says that 'The only way to be breakthrough as a brand is to be experimenting all the time.'[46]

Apart from the creative storytelling components of video for online engagement we should also look at pacing, vertical video, captions and super captions.

Pacing

When putting out a video ad, it's important to be succinct and to the point. People want to digest information quickly, especially if it's in the form of an advert.

Vertical video

Unless you're advertising on mobile-specific channels which specifically request vertical formats like Instagram/Facebook stories, Snapchat or YouTube shorts, it's best to stick to the horizontal format.

Captions

It's better to put subtitles on your videos, especially when advertising on platforms like Facebook, LinkedIn and Twitter, where people tend to watch without sound. This will make sure your messages are being heard, even when they aren't.

Super captions

Supplemental text – such as displaying short segments of the script on screen – is a popular way to deliver more information in a shorter time. So, it might be time to start getting creative with your text.

All of these tactics are a blueprint to what works on a level playing field. The most important thing is that you test and measure your video advertising with your own audience and potential customers.

As with all content, we want people to spend the maximum amount of time consuming the content, so we need to ensure we not only capture their attention at the beginning but leave them feeling like they gained something. Whether they got a laugh, felt sad or were educated, our tactics are to give, give, give somewhere between ten and twenty times before we can expect somebody to buy.

To start, we need a sixty- to ninety-second video. This could be a snippet of a larger video. We need to capture someone's attention in the first three seconds. This is generally done by grabbing the most exciting/informative/funny outtakes from the video they're about to watch and previewing them at the start of the video. We need to dive into the content quickly – without delay from logos or advertisements. We need to get into the meat of the story as quickly as possible.

Successful businesspeople tend to scoff at the thought of spending time and money producing video content without any expectation for financial gain, yet millions of YouTube creators do it every day. If you think you're going to create a video which cuts through the noise and you expect to make money overnight, you'd better think again. Nobody has ever had overnight success with anything, let alone video marketing.

The secret to creating any content – especially video – that makes money is by giving value to the user. If you want to sell more products, create informative, entertaining videos about the product. Talk about the complete list of features, ingredients, how it was made or what purpose it is perfect for and why. Talk about how, when and where to use the product.

Naming your product review video is important and you might go for 'best type of X' or 'product review' or 'how to use X'. All of these work well, so it's important not to just stop at one video; the last thing you want is people seeing your review or product comparison video and then searching elsewhere for the 'how to use' video or the 'complete buyer's guide' video. Consistency is key. If you only create one video and it gets a lot of views, your competitors will likely notice and see the opportunity to create more.

What if you want to sell your services but you work in the most boring industry, which nobody wants to know about? People usually want to know stuff and it's just a matter of digging through your most asked questions and starting there. If that fails, you can make 'rock stars' out of your clients and produce interviews.

How is this going to help you attract more clients? So long as you structure your content to answer the questions people want to hear most, and as a follow-up you have a low-cost service that is easy to purchase, you'll be winning.

Accounting is one of the less exciting industries and there isn't a great deal of content that's worth sharing. One exception to this is Xero, an online accounting software (founded in New Zealand in 2006) that majorly disrupted the market. The Xero YouTube channel, after a decade of existence, has 989 videos, over 57,000 subscribers (they had 7,000 in 2016) and over 11 million views.[47]

Even people who aren't on social media still watch plenty of YouTube videos, so keep that in mind when you're thinking about appealing to different demographics.

Almost any video production also has the potential to be redistributed as a podcast. Podcasting as a marketing tool is still really effective and high-profile entrepreneurs have mentioned podcasting as a good way to continue your audience engagement. Audio is a great way to engage, especially during people's downtime, when they're doing mundane tasks. Listening to podcasts can help those in lacklustre jobs get through the day.

The success of podcasting is surprising, but it's because it's so personal. It gives you a window into the people behind whatever industry you're talking about – what it's like to be in their shoes and their world.

Here are some methods you can use to produce your video and audio content.

Interview style

This is one of the easiest ways to produce content without feeling you're trying too hard or need to read perfectly from a script. It can be done in a studio or on location. The trick is to know just enough about your guest to be able to kick off the questioning and then listen for things that can trigger your next question.

The biggest lesson to learn is the listening part. You need to listen for those opportunities to take the conversation somewhere interesting and you need to keep your opinions to yourself as much as possible. If putting somebody else in the spotlight promotes them and their business, why would you bother?

Interviews break you out of your circle into other people's circles. They expand your network and potential popularity/notability within a community. Your questioning can be based on your values and the different perspectives and experience each person might have, which can support your own purpose. While the spotlight might be on someone else, you get to craft the topic of conversation for your own benefit and of course the benefit of the watchers/listeners.

Good conversation has a natural flow to it and if you're intrigued as the interviewer, time will fly by. I've had on-camera conversations that have lasted up to two and a half hours, which I could have sworn took a quarter of the time. There is nothing wrong with this because you have the potential to be able to cut up this content into multiple fifteen-second to one-minute snippets to distribute. Sharing the same story or interviewee repeatedly might get boring for the watchers but when you have multiple interviews in your arsenal to choose from, you'll have enough variety on a similar topic that people can see your values, purpose or cause shine through.

Talking head or presenter style

This could be the most daunting exercise a non-performer, shy CEO or introverted person could think of. The fear of public speaking is common and is known as glossophobia.

While you may be picturing thousands of people watching your content and judging you, you don't have to release a video if you or your peers believe it may not be right for public viewing. The hardest part is starting, and once you start talking to your smartphone camera you don't have to release every take – you can pick the best one or edit multiple together. Stutters can be edited out and the bits where your energy drops replaced with higher energy segments.

No one is perfect – especially not the first time – but having a crack and producing a video of you talking to camera can be amazing for not only your self-confidence but also your personal brand. Here are some tips for a successful take:

1. Warm up by doing some vocal chord and pronunciation exercises.

2. You don't have to do it off the cuff. Teleprompters allow you to script exactly what you want to say and when you practise over and over, people won't have a clue that you're reading. You can search for a teleprompter app on your smartphone or tablet, copy and paste your script, set up how quickly you're going to read and hit record.

3. Give all your energy to expressing your words and your positivity on the topic.

4. Do more than one take. Critique yourself and do another take, trying to improve on areas you feel need it.

5. Do at least ten takes. You'll get sick of saying the same thing over and over, feeling like you're not getting any better, but persistence is key.

6. Have your peers/editor/people you respect give you honest feedback and review the footage, remembering it's not meant to be perfect. Good enough can be good enough.

7. Edit it or transcribe it. If you didn't use the teleprompter and just presented off the cuff, transcribing your video can uncover some real content gold and maybe this time you'll just go with the transcription as a blog post.

8. Don't let your first time be the only time. Come back the next day and try again. Sleeping on these things can help you improve what you want to say.

Your topics should be kept to subject matter which closely relates to your expertise, passions, interests, cause, charity, values and purpose. This will help you speak from the heart rather than trying to force a discussion on a topic you may not be 'qualified' to speak on. I've made the mistake of chiming in on political debates and, while I have some interest in politics, it's not my area of expertise so I can end up looking stupid when it's just my opinion being expressed. Best to leave political, religious or sexual topics off camera. If you really feel the need to include them, save these discussions for interviews with qualified experts.

Presenter/narrator

If you find that having a talking head on camera could do with a little more pizazz, acting as the narrator or voiceover artist can greatly assist in pulling the best parts of each of your takes together. Try adding graphics, overlays or cutaway footage to your production as if you were presenting a slide deck presentation.

Treat this video like a weather segment on the news, where you might be presenting to camera and then showing cutaways to pictures of the surf, rain or a sunny day to support your story. You don't have to do it in the studio, but a green screen can offer you some flexibility with how you bring up graphics and special effects.

Video captions

According to a study by Verizon Media and Publicis, 69% of people report viewing video without sound in public places and 25% report viewing video without sound in private places.[48] If that's not enough to encourage you to put captions on your video content, we need to discuss scenarios you can relate to.

I'm going to go there again: the toilet. Nobody who's watching videos on the toilet wants to broadcast what they're doing, so people mute the sound on their device. Sometimes they forget, when they're in the toilet at a conference or seminar, and they end up spending a long time hidden in their cubicle, making sure nobody knows who was on their device while on the toilet.

Captions are useful in the office, on public transport or in a noisy environment. As I write, I'm sitting beside the beach at Burleigh Heads on the Gold Coast, with waves and wind preventing me from hearing properly.

I tend to watch movies, Netflix series and documentaries with captions on all the time. I hate missing a line or an important point due to my inadequate television speakers, background noise or the musical score. If my children are watching too much TV and aren't reading enough books, I encourage them to turn the sound off and read the captions.

Rev.com is my long-standing favourite tool for transcribing and getting captions for video content. You just have to drop the .srt file into your video and you've got a captioned video. In 2020, Rev.com released a burned-in captions option, which means you can just upload the video and receive the completed video with the captions burned in, without having to go back into your video editing software.[49]

Webinars

Webinars have become popular in the past ten years. They've surpassed the innovation phase but still exist midway to three-quarters through the early adoption phase. Webinars exploded in their popularity in 2020 and I expect this to increase dramatically in the next two years to the point that every B2B business will have them in their content arsenal.

Webinars are video content, which can be anything from a pre-recorded onstage panel discussion to a live talking head or slideshow presentation with a voiceover. Most webinars enable live questioning to be asked, whereby the presenter will respond live, and others are pre-recorded videos that should probably just be called a video.

Just like ebooks, white papers, case studies and research statistics, webinars generally have restricted access and you have to sign up in advance – either a few days or weeks ahead, or a few minutes ahead.

The ones that are happening in five or ten minutes are almost always pre-recorded but look and act as if they're live. They use similar software to everybody else, which enables the live questioning, but they're mostly just creating the illusion that they're live and they're really a webinar that is being regurgitated. Anybody who's gone to this kind of effort knows they have something compelling to tell you and are using every sales trick in the book to draw you in. I'm not saying this is bad but it errs on the side of sneaky and inauthentic, which in internet land means it's not going to have the longevity that being open and honest does.

I understand the psychology behind this – if it's live, I'm getting the first time, raw experience which could put me in front of the competition. If somebody really wants to see your live content, they'll make every effort to do so. The less trickery you use to get somebody to buy or sign up now, the more likely you are to build a sustainable business.

Instead of calling it a webinar, try calling it what it is – a live video or pre-recorded live video, demo, presentation or video course. This would do more to inform people what they're really going to get before they click the button.

As for running length, the thought of sitting and watching someone speak for an hour on a topic that's not live isn't going to convert users. Twenty minutes is probably the longest I would sit and watch a pre-recorded webinar.

If you're going to produce a webinar, making it more of a workshop means it is far more beneficial for the audience. They devote more time to thinking and completing the worksheets than they would just sitting there listening to you talk.

Email series

This is another way to gate content and drip-feed it to an audience on a certain day and time. Because so many people are using their email inbox for work as a way to dictate what they focus on each day, an email series can help to get on someone's radar consistently. Assuming the content is helpful to people looking to get work done, the email series is a good way to communicate but the content must be simple and easy to digest (taking two to five minutes).

Time of day is important when it comes to email, and being the first thing or the last thing on people's minds is the best way to time your emails. Given how busy my audience are, 5am is the best time for my emails to hit their inbox. Your audience could be different, but this is what you need to find out.

It's 5am and my potential customer has risen early to plan for a busy day. My content could be delivered in multiple ways. It might be an email series that says: 'Hey, you don't have to read this now, you can listen to this episode on my podcast while you're travelling to work, but if you like what you heard, feel free to forward this on to your colleagues who could also benefit, and maybe even bring it up as an agenda item at your next board meeting.'

We must use the different types of content at our disposal to get the attention of our ideal client. We must make it educational, inspirational or entertaining, or all three: the triple threat. We must make it easy to discover and easy to share.

CONTENT: Marketing Strategy

- List the types of media you'd like to use in your marketing.
- How many of these types do you think could be created per month?
- Are you going to educate, entertain or inspire your audience?
- Which persona(s) will your content appeal to?
- Which emotion are you going to attempt to tap into? Joy, sadness, fear, anger, disgust, surprise, trust, envy, love?

CONTENT: Marketing Campaign Plan

- List all the assets you need to create. Ideally these should each have due dates.
- Print assets will always come first, so be sure to factor in print advertising deadlines.

ELEVEN

Turn It On

By 'turn it on' I mean distribute the content via the channels where your audience is most likely to engage. Your content is no good sitting on your hard drive or your website if it's not getting seen.

Firstly, decide where this content is going to live. Where is its home? Blogs should be put on your own website, not a separate domain, LinkedIn article, Medium blog site or even sub-domain. They need to live somewhere like yourdomain.com/blog or a section called articles, news or insights. You should put excerpts of your blog onto your social media posts but the entire article should be on your website.

The other best place for your blog or article to live is on another reputable website such as those relating to news, education, the government or relevant sites with high traffic. Choose your locations carefully and make them count. Publishing more content on sites other than your own may affect the consistency of posts you publish on your site. This will not serve your brand well, so stick with the eighty/twenty rule, with 80% based on your website and 20% hosted elsewhere.

Let's talk about websites. The most common question when I start breaking this part down is: 'Are websites still valid?' The quick answer is yes. When we think about discoverability, we have to consider our distribution channels but we should not confine shareable content to just our own channels. Say you want to share what you've just found on Facebook with a colleague. Your colleague isn't on Facebook, so you send them a link and because the content is public they can most likely watch it in their browser, but that's where the sharing stops. Your friend doesn't know how to share it easily and we've broken any chance of the potential for multiple shares.

A link on a website is still the most universally understood and easiest way for people to share or come back to find your content. It's the home for all of your content, and nothing will expire or get lost in a sea of other content. It's easy to find via a Google or onsite search and over time your content's value only grows.

Your full-length and trailer videos should be hosted publicly on YouTube and the full-length version embedded within a blog post or landing page on your website. While Google continues to be the largest search engine in the world and lists YouTube videos within the search engine results pages, there's the possibility of having your videos found by other means than just landing on your site. This means more brand visibility and potential domination of the first page of Google, with more of your content hosted on your own page and on YouTube.

Getting traffic to your content requires you to share it. This can be done via:

- Email or electronic direct mail

- Posting to Google My Business

- Facebook, Instagram, LinkedIn, Twitter

- Forums, Reddit

- News publications, press releases

- YouTube, Vimeo, TikTok, Snapchat

- Podcasts, radio, TV

- SMS or MMS

Places to avoid:

- Directory websites
- Guest blogging websites with topics which do not relate to yours
- Publications that offer no link back to you or are blocked by paywalls/user subscription

Podcasts are on the rise. Currently there are 850,000, with over 30 million episodes between them.[50] Most marketers would say we need another podcast like we need a hole in the head, but they are a great opportunity for people to engage with you.

Earlier we discussed my potential client and how they're more than likely a busy C-level executive or manager who could be travelling a lot for work. They spend their weekends boating, lunching, going to the beach with their kids, but they also have time for the gym or doing odd jobs around the house. This is where podcasts come in. They make it possible for your ideal client to continue to spend time with you, versus somebody else, while they are performing another task.

Regardless of how many podcasts are out there, there is still a place for yours. If you can get your ideal client to consume your content in the way they want to consume it, you're another step closer to getting them as a customer.

TURN IT ON: Marketing Strategy

- List the channels you plan to distribute your content through.
- Indicate whether your campaigns will be monthly, quarterly, half yearly or yearly.
- Indicate the seasonal campaign months if they apply.

TURN IT ON: Marketing Campaign Plan

- Detail the dates on which you will distribute your content, using a content calendar or spreadsheet.
- Indicate to which channel each content asset will be distributed.

TWELVE

Ignite

When we were planning our Get Fact Up release of videos every week, we knew that posting content to social media was going to require us to ignite reach and engagement by applying an advertising spend. The spend was quite small but our targeting was great, and we managed to reach enough eyes that we got some great traction on Facebook and YouTube.

Once you've released your content into the world, your goal is to get as many eyes on it as possible for as long as possible. Organic reach and engagement have decreased greatly for content posted to Facebook in recent years. A couple of years ago, organic reach dropped to 1% and now only a fraction of a percent of your existing page followers are reached when you post. It's expected that all channels will go the same way, if they haven't already. We have to accept that to get greater reach and engagement on our content, we need paid advertising.

Paying to reach our target audience is not such a bad thing when we consider how powerful targeting on social media platforms like Facebook, Instagram and LinkedIn can be. LinkedIn advertising used to be expensive and offer little in the way of getting bang for your buck, especially when compared to Facebook and Instagram. This has improved a lot as of 2021.

Facebook owns Instagram and setting up advertisements for both channels via a single ad manager makes advertising across these platforms quite streamlined. But there's a catch. Platforms such as these are changing daily, and on many occasions in our years of advertising on these platforms we've seen options move or disappear from one ad manager account to another. The ad manager is definitely the right place to be managing your ads for Facebook and Instagram.

There are some powerful targeting options available:

- Location
- Interests
- Behaviour

- Connections
- Demographics

Location

Advertise in the cities, communities and countries where you want to do business. Choose your audience based on age, gender, education, job title and more. You can keep track of the types of people your ads are reaching, but Facebook will never share personally identifiable information about them.

Interests

Add interests and hobbies of the people you want your ad to reach – from organic food to action films – and make your targeted ads more relevant.

Behaviour

Target your ads based on consumer behaviours such as prior purchases and device usage.

Connections

Choose to include people who are connected to your Facebook page or event, or exclude them to find new audiences.

This ever-changing advertising environment is why I am not sharing detailed tactics on how to set up ads, but I will give a general outline as to what you may endure. Facebook has changed what parameters you can set during your audience targeting and will probably continue to introduce and remove features.

All posts should be made to your timeline and then promoted from there so that people can come back to find the ad if they want to. The content you share should be a combination of both 'pull' and 'push' style advertisements. Pull refers to blogs or microblogs (posting your blog directly into the platform's post area), native video (ie not an embedded YouTube or Vimeo video but one which is uploaded to the platform), and photos that are either striking or ambiguous to accompany your microblog or snippet of your full blog, which requires people to click the 'learn more'.

Push is the age-old advertising method of 'buy now' which rarely works unless you've nurtured your audience through a content funnel which educates, entertains or inspires them to really want your product/service.

Your initial goal for every post should be engagement. By getting people to engage with the post and ideally comment, you've created social proof that this content is worth consuming. Once this has been achieved, you can run another paid promotion of this same post which has an alternate objective, the most obvious being website traffic. This means directing people to read more, see more or download something from your website and, given that the post has some social engagement already, you should see a healthy click-through rate.

One important step before you embark on any Facebook advertising is to install a Facebook Pixel on your website. This will help you build an audience of visitors, which you can then use to target your promoted posts to. Sadly, time could be limited on this feature, as in early 2021 Apple released an IOS update affecting how Facebook receives and processes conversion events from the Facebook Pixel. Google Chrome will move towards disabling support for third-party cookies in 2022. Doubtless new workarounds will spring up in the years to come.

Customer lists are great for retargeting customers you have already done business with, are part of your email marketing subscription database and/or have made an enquiry or purchased something from your website.

For B2B marketing, the team at MeMedia love this type of list. If we are looking to engage on Facebook with somebody whose business email address we have, it's likely they are either a decision maker or influencer for their business because there is no differentiation between a work and personal email address. Alternatively, they could have a profile created just for work. This means they are probably using the same business email on Facebook that they've used to sign up to business-related newsletters.

For B2C marketing, the same theory applies. If they've used a personal email to sign up to a newsletter or enquire on your website about your product or service, they're also more inclined to have used that same email address for Facebook.

One challenge we sometimes find for Australian audiences is that we don't have the required level of reach to enable an ad to run using specific demographics and psychographics. It's important to be creative and test multiple audiences that still target your specific persona but use different parameters.

We have been running ads through LinkedIn for many years now and the engagement and click-through rates differ greatly among industries. I believe this is due to a combination of the adoption stage, when each industry has become aware of LinkedIn's benefits for business, and whether partnership and collaboration are encouraged. Given how good the organic reach of posting is on your personal profile, I would be inclined to increase your posting efforts here. But as with Facebook, LinkedIn will inevitably slowly decrease the organic reach, and funnel people and brands into their company pages and force people to pay to promote to get any engagement. So, enjoy it while it lasts.

Other channels worth paying to distribute content include advertorials on news websites. This is effectively paid PR and while they must state clearly that they are a paid placement, they can and do help increase your authority. They are a great addition to distribution via social media but it's important to ensure there is no disruption in your customers' journey, should they wish to visit your website from one of these advertorials. To combat this, make sure your website, products and services are up to date and that you have even better content on your website on the same topic as what has been released.

Another way to use paid advertising to promote traffic to your website is to use your content creation efforts to develop landing pages for Google advertising. You've done the keyword research and you know there is a high search volume for the topic of the content you've created. Google Adwords has the potential to perform well when used as a traffic source. This tactic is wasted if you don't have a strong call to action to access more information, sign up for special consideration or receive an offer on a purchase. You also need to watch your negative keywords closely on adwords, ensuring you're not spending money on searches which are clearly not associated with your product or service.

IGNITE: Marketing Strategy

- Content creation budget – how much are you going to invest into creating assets for your business overall or by month?
- Advertising spend budget for the year – broken down by month – here.

IGNITE: Marketing Campaign Plan

- What is the advertising budget assigned to this campaign to amplify its reach?
- Break down how the advertising budget will be spent, across each channel.

THIRTEEN

Verification

How do you know if your marketing efforts are leading your organisation down the right track if you aren't taking steps to measure your performance? During campaign execution, this is the most important step in your content marketing journey. Verifying that your team has done the work and validating whether your research, content creation, audience targeting, distribution and advertising were on point provides insights into where you might need to tweak one or all of your tactics.

In the past, when executing our methodology for several clients, we didn't always factor this step in. My team had either forgotten to do it or were requested not to do a certain task which was part of the monthly actions. Even though these clients had been with us for some years, the months where this didn't happen meant that steps in our methodology got overlooked, some Google advertising and social media advertising didn't happen and the marketing results were found to be lacklustre for those months.

Verifying you've done the work means you need weekly or fortnightly work in progress (WIP) meetings to ask these questions:

1. What keywords are we targeting?

2. Why are we targeting those keywords (ie search volume)?

3. What does our audience targeting look like?

4. What content are we creating?

5. When and where are we releasing that content?

6. Is our Google advertising fully functional?

7. What improvements have been made to our Google advertising and what do our conversions look like here?

8. What insights can we take from Google Adwords and inject back into our research and opportunity phases next time?

9. Where has our content been released and how is it performing?

You're going to need to get familiar with the following tools:

- Google Analytics

- Google Tag Manager

- Google Search Console

- Google Adwords

You will also need these tools to analyse your advertising on social media:

- Facebook Business Manager

- LinkedIn Ads Manager

- TikTok, Snapchat (ie the latest social media ads manager)

On day two of the month, your analytics for the previous month will be available for you to view via Google Analytics, Google Tag Manager and Google Search Console. By pulling together your WIP meeting notes and reports into one content marketing report, you'll have the data you need to establish insights into your marketing performance, enabling you to make informed decisions for the months ahead.

Notes within the end of month report as to how each traffic source is performing and reasons and opinions as to why they are performing in this way should be made by the data analyst on your team. These notes are for management, C-level or even the board to be able to understand what drove the changes in your metrics.

This report must be read and signed off by all parties who are active in the marketing to confirm that they were responsible for the activities which took place and that they understand the impact of those activities. This empowers each team member to understand how one change on the website or advertising might affect positive or negative movement in traffic towards your physical store, phone or inbox.

Activities to verify

- Expected amount of content was created.

- All content was turned on and ignited.

  - Verified by screenshots or reports of the results for each.

- Other 'always on' advertising (eg Google Adwords) was fully functional, managed and optimised.

  - Broad keywords are monitored to ensure they're not using the entire budget.

  - Exact keywords should have an increased budget.

- Negative keywords were reviewed and added.

- Ad copy was reviewed and tweaked according to what the top two to three best-performing ads are.

- Landing pages are working without error.

Metrics to validate

- SEO (website)

  - Average number of pages viewed

  - Average time on site

  - New vs returning visitors

  - Traffic source

  - Keywords being found

  - Bounce rate

  - Number of conversions to a lead or sale

  - Conversion rate

- Adwords

  - Average cost per click (CPC) or cost per 1,000 impressions (CPM)

  - Average cost per acquisition (CPA)

  - Clicks vs impressions

- – Number of conversions from views to click

- – Number of conversions from click to lead

- – Conversion rate

- Social media advertising

  - – Reach vs engagement

  - – Video view-throughs

  - – Average CPC or CPM

  - – Clicks

  - – Conversion rate

Conversions and leads

Conversion rates are always one of the main topics of interest on reports and while we marketers would love to have the full picture on our conversions from marketing to sales, we don't always get this, so we stick to discussing the conversion rates of traffic to a lead.

A website lead is when you obtain somebody's information from the website to be able to follow up with them, and generally comes in the form of a web form submission, a click to call, a content gated white paper/ebook download or a signup to an online course or ticketed event. Online courses and events could also be considered sales conversions but in modern content marketing, courses and events are most commonly used to give potential customers a small taste of what you're capable of, so that you can sell them into something bigger.

A sale is a conversion, but just getting people to navigate to where you want them to go on the website could also be classed as a conversion. According to Tim Ash, author of *Landing Page Optimization*, we can only keep four items in our non-rehearsed memory, which means you need to limit the choices available to your users when they're visiting your page.[51] This could apply to anything on your website, such as selecting the right section to navigate to, or selecting a product category, and maybe even which price package is best among a sea of pricing packages. Cutting the options down on your website to no more than four will help funnel those users into the areas you want them and create more conversions.

We want to make the available choices obvious. This can be done by adding a sash to one of the four pricing options or even increasing the height of the one you wish the customer to choose. For navigation through to parts of your website or shopping cart, you might have black and white descriptive photos and one in full colour, promoting visual bias.

Let's take another look at the price packaging options and show how manipulating context and order can help increase conversions. If you look at your four package options with prices included, then change the order of them from highest on the left to lowest on the right, this can give your middle or basic packages a psychological edge.

When considering category and navigation structure, pushing your most popular on-page visual buttons around so that they are visible in one view without scrolling, and not exceeding four options, can assist the visitor.

Prices are a pain for website visitors. If you offer price packaging options, simply removing the dollar figure from your price packages but including the currency you're trading in could give those packages another psychological edge.

Conversion rates are important because they are numbers we can bank on. If we find our email marketing is getting a 20% open rate, a 1.8% click-through rate and another 1% conversion to a lead (filling out a form), we may have to increase our subscriber numbers or improve our conversion rate to get more leads. Email is difficult to increase your conversion rate on, but consistent content marketing can help convert dormant subscribers over time, as long as your content is valuable, you stay on topic and don't annoy people by being too frequent, which can lead to high unsubscribe rates.

Consistency with email marketing means fulfilling your promise from the beginning. Tell people when they sign up that they're going to get an email every day or every Monday morning or on the first Monday of every month. This way they're not surprised. They expect your email and as it's valuable to your potential customer, they'll look forward to it.

VERIFICATION: Marketing Strategy

Your strategy should detail what indicates a successful three-, six- or twelve-month marketing campaign. For example:

- Traffic to the website has increased from X to Y.
- Bounce rate has decreased by X%.
- Leads per month have increased from X to Y.
- Google ranking for the top four to six keywords which were of high search volume is within the top ten positions.
- Increase in followers/likes.
- Average engagement rate has increased.
- Increase in email database subscribers, open rates and click-throughs.
- Video views average X per month.
- Podcast downloads reach X per month.
- Sales have increased from X to Y per month.

Verification: Campaign Plan

- What strategic key performance indicators does this campaign impact?

Verification: Marketing Execution

The PROACTIVE framework should be used as a checklist to confirm all activities were undertaken according to the current campaign plan.

- **Purpose:** the purpose of the campaign was upheld and successful. The values were upheld and so was the tone of voice.
- **Research:** the keywords and phrases used resulted in quality content output.
- **Opportunity:** the platform requirements were met and performance was as expected.
- **Audience:** the audience targeting was on point (or needs to be adjusted).
- **Content:** all content assets were created.
- **Turn on:** distribution to planned channels was performed.
- **Ignite:** paid amplification was used for each content/ asset.
- **Verification:** we completed this checklist and validated the results.
- **Evolve:** we know what actions are required to evolve this campaign and have executed those actions or have them planned to execute in the next PROACTIVE campaign plan.

FOURTEEN

Evolve

I f we don't evolve, how can we become better? During
your strategy creation, you may anticipate that you'll
need to evolve your marketing because of seasonality
or a well-known occurrence within your industry. It's
important to make note of this to inform the marketers
that they will need to make adjustments to their campaigns at these times.

During the marketing campaign execution, taking
insights from this month's activities will allow you to
make improvements to your previous content/cam-
paign. With the insights from Google Analytics, start
with the website and any content/SEO updates that
could be made to improve the leading key performance
indicators (KPIs) which will affect our lagging KPIs,
such as improving our Google organic ranking.

It's not best practice to create new content which says the same thing over and over. We need to find ways to improve our existing content and this is not only appealing to people who may have already read and enjoyed the blog the first time, but also to Google.

The leading SEO KPIs you're looking to impact are:

- Average time on site

- Returning visitors

- Bounce rate

- Average number of pages viewed

The key activities which will impact these leading KPIs should be ever evolving. Remember that making improvements to your content is not always about pleasing the search robot – improving your user experience can and does improve your potential for better Google rankings. Try these activities:

- Insert links from within your paragraph text to new blogs you've created or to product or services pages.

- Make updates and timestamp those updates at the beginning of the blog.

- Encourage unique, user-generated content such as comments.

- Ensure that your technical SEO is up to scratch and make tweaks where necessary.

- Update your meta title, title of your blog and/or headings if you've discovered better keywords which fit with your keyword research, always making sure you mention the previous post title beneath the title in smaller text.

- Plan to create an infographic or video which could support or better explain or entertain the readers of your blog post.

Giving reasons for people to return to your website relates to the last point, which directly impacts the evolution of where you turned on your content last time and where you ignited it. If we're able to reach out to the same audience who showed interest and activity on the advertising we produced last time, we can re-advertise to them and inform them that we have 'updated content'.

Once we have created a blog which has been well received, the most logical step is usually to create an infographic, which we post into the first half of the blog. We then redistribute and advertise this with 'infographic', 'visual guide' or 'step by step' in the blog title. People love them.

The more single-page content is updated with unique content or refers you to other similar pages, the more Google recalls those pages and updates its ranking.

We once did an infographic for a bariatric surgeon to visually explain the body mass index (BMI) scale and how even a muscular, fit person could be deemed obese by the index. Not only did this receive a lot of traffic and attention, it helped take our client's organic Google ranking from page five to position number one for the generic search term 'bariatric surgery' in Australia.

The other content styles should help you improve your content and engagement when you update existing content and lead people to new and improved media.

Bounce rates are when somebody lands on a page of your website and then exits the website, by either clicking 'back' or closing the tab/window and ending the session. Anything between 55% and 70% bounce rate is considered high and over 70% is extreme. Decreasing the bounce rate is the same as saying we want to increase the conversion rate of people clicking through to the next page. This could mean your blog has a 'register now' or 'donate now' button but it may also have links to previous blogs or your product or service pages, which also have calls to action on them.

Increasing the time on site is also about getting people to click through to another page. The event of them clicking provides a secondary timestamp for Google Analytics to track so that it has a start and end time of how long they were on a specific page. Without the second click, somebody could spend all day looking at a page, close the tab or window and Google Analytics wouldn't know how long they've been there and instead would class this as a bounce.

It's important to remember that if your conversions meet your expectations, you may not need to adjust your ad, but in most cases we rarely nail it first time. Now that we've made some improvements to the content (landing page), we can look to improve the traffic driver(s) to the page. The first one is our social media advertising, where we need to:

• Improve the call to action (CTA) of our ad

• Update the ad thumbnail or video

• Improve our audience targeting

Using Facebook as our example, they only offer us generic CTA buttons to choose from and these change depending on what the purpose of your ad is. Facebook categorises these under awareness consideration and conversion. It could be to get brand awareness, video views, traffic to your website or catalogue purchases.

The first time I distribute a video to Facebook, I post it to my timeline, and use post engagement as my marketing objective. This adds to the number of likes and comments I get on the post, which often means we've built social proof around this content being worthy of attention. When we come back to evolve the marketing objective the second time, we would use traffic to drive people to the blog on the website. Traffic has a number of different CTA button options, such as:

- No button

- Book now

- Contact us

- Donate now

- Download

- Get showtimes

- Learn more

- Listen now

- Request time

Updating the graphic or video on your ads can be a good idea but if we already have an ad people are successfully engaging with, it's best not to change this. If you've already got great engagement with your post, this is the social proof you want and just changing the CTA is a great way to leverage this engagement.

EVOLVE: Marketing Strategy

- Will our campaign evolve?
- If so, how is this anticipated?

Evolve: Marketing Campaign Plan

- Indicate the dates when we will need to evolve and a short sentence to explain what.

FIFTEEN

PROACTIVE Summary

Congratulations, you made it this far. If you're a person of action, you've probably taken one to two months to execute the methodology to create your strategy. When looking at repeating this methodology on a monthly basis, use the marketing campaign plan notes under each of the nine steps.

Your strategy should be ever evolving, checking in on your purpose and values. Your keyword research and competitor analysis will need to evolve with your content output. Opportunities will be found when you keep doing investigative work and making tweaks or improvements. You may find that PRO only needs to be reviewed and improved every three months, whereas ACTIVE will be more consistent.

If you're feeling overwhelmed by the activities and wondering how you're going to do them all, you may be relieved to know that they are generally done by a team and rarely done by one individual. In the next chapter, I'll break down some example team structures for you.

This book was written between 2019 and 2021. I hope and expect that new and improved ways to reach audiences will arise beyond those I've outlined here.

When you 'turn on' and 'ignite' your content, the tactics are meant as a guide only. They're meant to show you that when you undertake your advertising on LinkedIn, Instagram, TikTok and so on, the fundamentals should remain the same. Each platform will have different features but, given how they've evolved, the principles of distribution and advertising will stay relevant. LinkedIn is very successful at the moment for turning on your content, and advertising on LinkedIn can only get better. Just do organic distribution on your personal profile, and test the advertising every few months with new audience targeting to see if there are any improvements.

Content marketing is about slowly building trust with your audience. Gaining quick wins is not what this is about, and quick wins don't help you build a sustainable business. By investing in content marketing, we are investing in assets which work together to build your brand's value over time. Stopping is not an option. We have had clients come to us, implement the twelve-month content marketing campaign, see their business improve and then believe they could stop. They changed to radio advertising – completely ignored their content creation and distribution efforts – and after three months their website traffic and lead flow were back to where they were when they first engaged us. I've seen this happen repeatedly, a stark reminder that consistency is vital.

Once you're ahead of your competition or even just a little ahead of where you were, don't stop. Keep going and if you get to the point where you feel you've plateaued, add other marketing and advertising methods on top of your content marketing such as doubling down on the landing pages and lead generation ads. Don't replace it. Your content will serve you well in the long term.

SIXTEEN

Teams

Building teams since 2006 has been a privilege. It's one of the greatest achievements of my career. I've been able to constantly build teams for new clients and new marketing campaigns. I have attracted some very skilled people who have evolved continuously in the world of marketing. Each has become more knowledgeable about specific aspects of web development, marketing and advertising than I have.

Our knowledge sharing for the past few years has made us all better marketers together than we are alone. I was once a lone multimedia contractor and being a jack of all trades makes it hard to master one. I built a team of experts around me and the results improved.

A well-functioning, collaborative team should behave as one person, capable of using both sides of their brain. When they're in flow, they connect with one another at supersonic speeds, as if they were nodes within the brain.

Multi-tasking is an important factor to consider, because it is impossible to focus our attention on more than one task at a time and do them all in an effective manner. It's only when we divide the tasks among a team that we are able to execute multiple tasks at once.

My career has been made up of two parts. My early years were all about tactical execution. Being the designer, programmer, developer of ecommerce websites, photographer, camera operator, video editor, animator, Google and social media advertiser, SEO and data analyst. After seven or eight years, I was starting to burn out.

All of the above activities came to be known as content marketing but the biggest thing that had changed was how consistent we needed to be. In the early days (pre-social media), I recall launching an ecommerce website and getting orders on day one, with zero advertising spend. As long as the website was indexed in Google, that was enough. By 2007, it took a week for the first orders to start coming through and since the global financial crisis in 2008, it's taken months to get that first sale for an unknown brand with no pre-launch marketing.

It's more competitive now than it ever was and the volume of work which needs to be done to make an impact has increased. The amount of content you can create influences your frequency of distribution and advertising and while your goal is to turn on new content every day, unless you have a team to do this, you're going to burn out in weeks.

Consistency is everything in business, and especially in content marketing. I often liken it to making a snowball – if the ball stops rolling, it's not going to grow. If it's left stagnant too long it is more than likely going to melt. Let's start with the end in mind and build a team that's capable of such activity. One that can be scaled to have a skills redundancy matrix that can protect you from coming up short on your marketing efforts.

Start by looking at your marketing team organisation chart and listing the roles as if one person would be doing each.

- CEO
- CFO
- COO
- Project manager

- Marketing director

- Sales director

- Customer service manager

- Data analyst

- Back-end developer

- Front-end developer/SEO

- Videographer and editor

- Graphic designer

- Copywriter

- Social media marketer

- Public relations specialist

For most businesses, creating a team of this magnitude is a pipe dream. We need to look at how we can couple roles with their most compatible skillset. If you're a small business, it's highly likely the COO, CEO and CFO are the same person. They may also encompass the project manager and marketing director roles.

Then there is the possibility of coupling the data analyst with the back-end and front-end developers. Combine the videographer, editor and graphic designer and combine the customer service manager, copywriter, social media marketer and public relations specialist.

The smallest effective team you can build is made up of four people. As your company grows, it makes sense to start dividing these roles back into their individual skillsets, where everyone from the sales director down could be duplicated to meet demand.

Hiring your team just based on their skillset isn't always the best way to keep a team in tune. Some say we should hire based on attitude, not skillset, because skills can always be learned. While I agree with this statement, I'd like to add the importance of shared values.

One of the areas where my teams fell apart was when work/life pressure got a little too much and it was a lack of shared values that ultimately made these teams disintegrate. Shared values are more important than we realise. The leader must share three values with each team member to be relatable. If the leader has a single value which is an absolute non-negotiable, it's important that each team member possesses this value. This is a lesson I have learned the hard way; when mistakes were made and I had to manage performance, the team members I didn't share values with ended up leaving.

Respect has always been my number one value. I adopted this from my dad and also my martial arts teachers. I have always been the first to give respect and when it has not been reciprocated, that's when I find it difficult to continue with a relationship. This is my example of the one value I must share with everybody I spend time with to build a solid foundation on which to share other values and enjoy working or living together.

Honesty is another one of my non-negotiable values. Patience, trust, accountability and responsibility are high on my list but none of these can trump the importance of having fun. Non-negotiable values remain pretty consistent throughout life, but like all values that doesn't mean they can't or shouldn't change, especially when you've experienced some kind of adversity which puts the emphasis on these values into question.

Apart from your non-negotiable values, you should be able to adjust and identify different combinations of your value set with other individuals' values. Is there a magic number of values a team member must be aware of for us to find our three values within? I suggest that each team member should be able to choose fifteen values. Other team members and leaders should then be able to find three within the fifteen which are shared.

Sometimes we feel we're not speaking the same language as our team members. Values are the moral fibres which help us understand each other and are the key to harmonious and long-term relationships. The words used to describe our values are often not enough to explain the behaviours we accept and don't accept within our team. Often each person interprets the meaning of words to be different from others' understanding.

Discussing these behaviours, documenting them and revisiting them with the team during the monthly PROACTIVE marketing verification meeting can help with not only your marketing but also your company culture.

Conclusion

Purpose and values were the elements missing from earlier versions of my marketing methodology. Had I not gone through a period of adversity, I wouldn't be here talking about what a change this has made to my life and the clients I work with. Purpose inspires everything and everyone.

The overarching belief behind this book was that all organisations that wish to succeed beyond the 2030s must have a purpose beyond profit, then must build their brand on top of this purpose.

In order to understand our brand purpose, we must first understand our values, for If we are to relate to others, we must first be able to relate to ourselves.

Who inspires you? Do they have big dreams? Don't be afraid to dream big. Does it make you feel anxious that you might never achieve this enormous dream? That's OK. You're not alone. The media focus on big purposes solving big problems, but there are plenty of smaller problems worth solving that are still rewarding.

Remember your personal purpose and understand what your next step is going to be or should be according to your strategy. If you don't have a strategy, that's your next step. It takes sparks to build a fire and sometimes the timber is wet. You may need to find new timber and start with smaller kindling, beneath a shelter, out of the rain. In other words, take some time to clear your mind and make a start on your purpose/strategy.

Entrepreneurs are notorious for running off on tangents with new ideas that they want to pursue. Usually when they're at their busiest. This would be an opportune time to recognise the simplicity and power of the PROACTIVE Planner: sketch out a quick nine-box grid and process the new ideas into a PROACTIVE plan. If the idea still sounds good after going through this process, then maybe it's worth creating the full-blown PROACTIVE strategy.

It is important to continue the research to ensure we're not operating in a vacuum of our own thoughts and beliefs. Creating a strategy is a true test of an entrepreneur's patience and will also help you find out whether you've got the determination to see this idea through.

Be proactive, not reactive. Don't rely on a single channel or 'trick' to maintain your business long-term. Develop your strategy and concern yourself – ideally your team – with executing it.

Consistency, cadence and timing are what you need.

Don't be disheartened if you feel you've been saying the same thing over and over and you think, 'Surely people will be sick of hearing this.' People have only just started to listen.

Invest in creating assets more than you invest in liabilities. Seek to engage your audience with assets that have emotion and adopt your values, so they remember how you made them feel.

If you've been executing your marketing for some time and you're either not getting traction or you've reached a plateau, then this is the time to check in with your values, purpose and the problem you're solving.

Ask yourself if the content assets you're creating are being produced in-line with your values? Are your content assets delivering what you promised? Really? What value are your customers getting from your content?

If the value your customers get from your content is not educational, inspirational or entertaining and lacks emotional depth then there is an opportunity for it to be reworked.

I hope you use the PROACTIVE framework to create your marketing strategy and continually question the efficacy of your marketing efforts.

There is so much to learn from taking action. So please, be proactive and above all, don't stop evolving.

References

1 World Health Organization, *The World Health Report 2001: Mental health – new understanding, new hope* (WHO, 2001), www.who.int/whr/2001/en, accessed 9 April 2021

2 Human Rights Law Centre, 'Prime Minister's plan to outlaw environment boycott campaigns is deeply concerning' (HRLC, 2019), www.hrlc.org.au/news/2019/11/1/prime-ministers-plan-to-outlaw-environment-boycott-campaigns-is-deeply-concerning, accessed 9 April 2021

3 C Hughes, 'Bushfires in Australia: statistics and facts' (Statista, 2021), www.statista.com/topics/6125/bushfires-in-australia, accessed 9 April 2021

4 UNICEF, 'The formative years' (UNICEF, 2019), https://data.unicef.org/wp-content/uploads/2019/09/Formative-Years-ECD-Brochure-EN.pdf, accessed 9 April 2021

5 S Godin, *This is Marketing: You can't be seen until you learn to see* (Penguin, 2018)

6 Oxford English Dictionary, 'Culture' (OED, no date), www.lexico.com/definition/culture, accessed 12 April 2021

7 C Hackett and D McClendon, 'Christians remain world's largest religious group, but they are declining in Europe' (Pew Research Center, 2017), www.pewresearch.org/fact-tank/2017/04/05/christians-remain-worlds-largest-religious-group-but-they-are-declining-in-europe, accessed 11 February 2019

8 J Peterson, *12 Rules for Life: An antidote to chaos* (Allen Lane, 2018)

9 JF Demartini, *The Values Factor: The secret to creating an inspired and fulfilling life* (Berkley, 2013)

10 J Peterson, *12 Rules for Life: An antidote to chaos* (Allen Lane, 2018)

11 Y Chouinard and V Stanley, *The Responsible Company: What we've learned from Patagonia's first 40 years* (Patagonia, 2012)

12 Patagonia, 'Company history' (Patagonia, no date), www.patagonia.com/company-history, accessed 12 April 2021

13 Y Chouinard, 'A letter from our founder' (1% for the Planet, 2020),
    www.onepercentfortheplanet.org/stories/a-letter-from-yvon
    -chouinard, accessed 12 April 2021

14 S McChrystal, *Team of Teams: New rules of engagement for a complex
    world* (Penguin, 2015)

15 E Morphy, 'This is Tim Cook's Apple: a company where "Mini-
    Steve" gets the axe', *Forbes* (30 October 2012), www.forbes.com/sites
    /erikamorphy/2012/10/30/this-is-tim-cooks-apple-a-company
    -where-mini-steve-gets-the-axe, accessed 12 April 2021

16 L Kahney, *Tim Cook: The genius who took Apple to the next level*
    (Portfolio, 2019)

17 J Cross, 'Tim Cook on Apple's values, regulation, excessive phone
    use, health, and more', *Macworld* (23 April 2019), www.macworld
    .com/article/232692/tim-cook-on-apple-values-regulation-excessive
    -phone-use-health-and-more.html, accessed 12 April 2021

18 PwC, *Putting Purpose to Work: A study of purpose in the workplace*
    (PwC, 2016), www.pwc.com/us/en/about-us/corporate
    -responsibility/assets/pwc-putting-purpose-to-work-purpose
    -survey-report.pdf, accessed 12 April 2021

19 S Czarnecki, 'Eight in 10 consumers say they're more loyal to
    purpose-driven brands', *PRWeek* (30 May 2018), www.prweek.com
    /article/1466208/eight-10-consumers-say-theyre-loyal-purpose
    -driven-brands-cone, accessed 12 April 2021

20 S Sinek, *The Infinite Game: How great businesses achieve long-lasting
    success* (Portfolio, 2019)

21 RW Emerson, 'Self-reliance' in *Essays: First series* (self-published,
    1841)

22 I Kwai, 'Donations are pouring into Australia. Now what?' *New
    York Times* (18 January 2020), www.nytimes.com/2020/01/18/world
    /australia/fires-donations-help.html, accessed 12 April 2021

23 E Ritvo, 'The Neuroscience of Giving', Psychology Today (24 April
    2014), www.psychologytoday.com/au/blog/vitality/201404/the
    -neuroscience-giving, accessed 12 April 2021

24 W Isaacson, *Steve Jobs* (Simon & Schuster, 2011)

25 E Tolle, *A New Earth: Awakening to your life's purpose* (Viking, 2005)

26 W Isaacson, *Steve Jobs* (Simon & Schuster, 2011)

27 W Isaacson, *Steve Jobs* (Simon & Schuster, 2011)

28 A Fothergill and J Hughes, *David Attenborough: A life on our planet*
    (Altitude Film Entertainment/Netflix, 2020)

29 JF Demartini, *The Values Factor: The secret to creating an inspired and
    fulfilling life* (Berkley, 2013)

30 S McChrystal, *Team of Teams: New rules of engagement for a complex
    world* (Penguin, 2015)

31 S Sinek, *The Infinite Game: How great businesses achieve long-lasting
    success* (Portfolio, 2019)

32 B Walker and H Pene, *Cashed Up: 7 steps to pull more money, time and happiness from your business* (Inspire, 2018)

33 T Smith, Successful Advertising (self-published, 1885)

34 Google, *Zero Moment of Truth* (Google, 2011), www.thinkwithgoogle .com/marketing-strategies/micro-moments/zero-moment-truth, accessed 20 April 2021

35 M Cutts, 'The decay and fall of guest blogging for SEO', Matt Cutts blog (20 January 2014), www.mattcutts.com/blog/guest-blogging, accessed 13 April 2021

36 D Davies, 'Meet the 7 most popular search engines in the world', *Search Engine Journal* (3 March 2021), www.searchenginejournal.com /seo-101/meet-search-engines, accessed 20 April 2021

37 J Allen, 'SEOs strike out as Google encrypts signed-in search data', *Search Engine Watch* (19 October 2011), www.searchenginewatch.com /2011/10/19/seos-strike-out-as-google-encrypts-signed-in-search -data, accessed 20 April 2021

38 R Honeywill, 'Millennials: a giant generational hoax?' Roy Morgan blog (30 May 2016), www.roymorgan.com/findings/6792 -millennials-a-giant-generational-hoax-201605030703, accessed 20 April 2021

39 Deloitte, *The 2016 Deloitte Millennial Survey: Winning over the next generation of leaders* (Deloitte, 2016), www2.deloitte.com/content /dam/Deloitte/global/Documents/About-Deloitte/gx-millenial -survey-2016-exec-summary.pdf, accessed 20 April 2021

40 A Maina, '20 Popular Social Media Sites Right Now', Small Business Trends (4 May 2016), https://smallbiztrends.com/2016/05/popular -social-media-sites.html, accessed 24 May 2021

41 5WPR, '5WPR 2020 Consumer Culture Report', 5W Public Relations (20 February 2020), www.5wpr.com/new/wp-content/uploads/pdf /5W_consumer_culture_report_2020final.pdf, accessed 24 May 2021

42 G Pickard-Whitehead, 'Millennials Still Using Facebook More Than Any Other Social Media Site', Small Business Trends (6 February 2020), https://smallbiztrends.com/2020/02/2020-consumer-culture -report.html, accessed 24 May 2021

43 C Bulbul, N Gross, S Shin and J Katz, *When the path to purchase becomes the path to purpose* (Google, 2014), https://think.storage .googleapis.com/docs/the-path-to-purpose_articles.pdf, accessed 20 April 2021

44 5WPR, '5WPR 2020 Consumer Culture Report', 5W Public Relations (20 February 2020), www.5wpr.com/new/wp-content/uploads/pdf /5W_consumer_culture_report_2020final.pdf, accessed 24 May 2021

45 S Sinek, *Start With Why: How great leaders inspire everyone to take action* (Penguin, 2009)

46 B Janacek Reeber and K McKesten, 'Google's Unskippable Labs has run over 250 video ad experiments. Learn their approach', Think with Google (March 2020), www.thinkwithgoogle.com/intl/en

-aunz/marketing-strategies/video/video-tests-and-experiments, accessed 24 May 2021

47 Xero Accounting Software channel (YouTube), www.youtube.com /channel/UCIDB-mYEzMjGRhpHF6VvzLQ, accessed 20 May 2021

48 Verizon Media, 'Break the sound barrier with digital video captioning' (Verizon Media, 2019), www.verizonmedia.com /insights/break-sound-barrier-with-digital-video-captioning, accessed 15 April 2021

49 Rev, 'Announcing: open captions (burned-in captions)', Rev blog (17 August 2020), www.rev.com/blog/announcing-open-captions -burned-in-captions, accessed 21 April 2021

50 Y Lin, 'Ten powerful podcast statistics you need to know in 2021', Oberlo blog (4 January 2021), www.oberlo.co.uk/blog/podcast -statistics, accessed 21 April 2021

51 T Ash, *Landing Page Optimization: The definitive guide to testing and tuning for conversions* (Sybex, 2008)

Acknowledgements

I'm grateful I have the opportunity to thank so many people who've helped me get here. My only fear is that I will forget someone who is truly deserving of being thanked and is left off these pages.

The biggest thanks go to my parents, Geoffrey and Rosemary Hogan, for giving me the best start in life any child could ask for and encouraging me to try new things like soccer, piano and saxophone, dance, martial arts and surfing, and sending me to great schools where I made lifelong friends. Most of all, I thank you both for encouraging me to never give up.

To my older sisters, Sharon and Kim, you've been the two extra mother figures I needed to mould me into the man I am. Without your influence, I'm sure my confidence with and my empathy towards women would not have developed as well as it has.

To my wife, Amy, who's been my rock for over half my life, giving me reassurance and purpose to be a loving husband and father to three girls, Maya, Eve and Quinn.

To my children, for helping me understand what it means to be a father. I've had to improve myself and even though I may feel grown, I've still got plenty more growth left in me.

Thank you, Mark and Karen Paton, for having such a beautiful and strong-willed daughter for me to marry. Thank you, Karen, for being my number one Facebook fan.

To Stacey and Yogi, your loving support is always noticed and appreciated.

To the Archdeacon family, specifically Donna. Your words of encouragement have meant a lot in the final days of writing this book and helped me push through to the end.

I've mentioned people I've met throughout my career that have made the most impact on me, but Leigh Kelson takes the cake as the best mentor any business owner could ask for. Working with Leigh was one of the best experiences I've had in what it takes to build a business, pitch, sell and grow it. Leigh either operates at zero or ten, nothing in between. If he looks like he is sitting idle, he's researching, connecting the dots and using the strength of his network to discover answers to questions he doesn't already have. Leigh believes in solving problems worth solving. He's discovered that the best way to motivate oneself is to find a big problem and start solving it. Much of what I lacked in business became evident because Leigh didn't hold back on his observations and gave it to me straight. I've learned so much from you, Leigh – thank you.

Thank you to my sensei and friend, Jamie Mac Aninch, for being yet another mentor in my life who's also taught me the 'never say die' attitude. We've shared a passion for martial arts and mobility training that started at a young age and I'm grateful for being taught the importance of learning an ancient warrior art and making it applicable to being a modern-day warrior. A warrior who understands light and dark, softness and strength. Domo Arigato.

To those MeMedia team members who helped shape me, our clients and our company. Thank you to Jenna Faint, my first ever employee, for believing in me and MeMedia for your seven-year term. Kevin Allison, for being the longest-standing employee and my rock within the business. Steve Williams, for also being a long-standing supporter and being a creative guy who never shies away from a creative challenge. I'm equally grateful to all the other team members who've taught me life lessons, without which I would not be the man I am today.

To the clients who got MeMedia off the ground and to the long-standing clients who've stayed. Both I and the team at MeMedia have enjoyed working with you all and hope this continues for many more years.

Thank you to Michael Clark from Dent Global for encouraging me to take on the challenges of the Key Person of Influence course, and for introducing me to Rethink Press. Thanks also to Daniel Priestley for inspiring me many years ago to want to become an author.

The Author

Chris Hogan is a leading strategic content marketer, building brands on purpose. He has spent over twenty years working within Australia and internationally and is the founder of MeMedia Marketing Agency, headquartered in Burleigh Heads on the Gold Coast, Australia.

He is well known for being the host of *The PROACTIVE Podcast* and developing an easy-to-implement marketing framework, helping his clients be more strategic and achieve smooth, reliable, sustainable growth.

A passionate advocate for being purpose-led, Chris hopes this book means he will be able to help more founders and visionaries harness their purpose and make an impact across the globe.

You can find more information about Chris on his website ⊕ www.chrishogan.com.au and see his updates on LinkedIn here: in www.linkedin.com/in/chrishoges and also on instagram ⊙ @chrishoges

All of the downloads for this book are available at ⊕ www.proactivemarketing.co.

To stay up to date with PROACTIVE downloads, events, podcasts and content, you can subscribe to the mailing list or follow ⊙ @pro.act.ive on Instagram.